WHAT THEY DON'T TEACH YOU IN SALES SCHOOL

-Make selling a career –not a job!

Learn to become a seasoned professional without
spending twenty years doing it

SCOTT J. DUNKEL

ISBN: 147915041X

ISBN 13: 9781479150410

Library of Congress Control Number: 2012915240

CreateSpace Independent Publishing Platform
North Charleston, South Carolina

Table of Contents

Acknowledgments v

Foreword vii

Introduction.. xi

1) Developing Your Annual Business Plan....................................1

2) How Well Do You Know Your Product or Service? 17

3) Know Who You're Calling On 29

4) The Art of Listening 43

5) Step Out of Your Comfort Zone and Sell at All Levels................53

6) Presentation Skills/Proposal Generation 65

7) The Financial Sale/How to Manufacture Business.......................77

8) Working with Sales Management..89

9) Selection of Resources...97

10) The Business Relationship/Entertainment..............................109

11) Sales Execs Don't Close Large Transactions — Clients Buy
    Because…? 119

12) Handling a Lost Sale/What Can You Learn? 127

13) Account Management/Competition..137

14) The Sales Triangle/ Management-Sales-Clients, or Balancing the
    Three-Legged Stool 151

15) Thinking Outside the Box 169

16) Career Changes Both In and Out of Your Industry 183

17) Putting It All Together..193

    Appendix: Five Universal Sales Truths.......................................201

    About the Author 205

Acknowledgments

This book project has been an absolute blessing. It has provided an opportunity to reconnect with many of the folks I worked with and sold to over the last thirty years. It has also offered the opportunity to meet with folks in other industries to get input on the various topics in the book.

I'm extremely grateful to the following individuals who helped make this book a reality. They are, in alphabetical order:

Kevin Apperson, Sam Bennet, Phil Burgess, Mike Burke, Pat Daniels, John DiPierro, Bob Farrow, Jody Giles, MJ Golibart, Don Hilliard, Frank Jerd, Jim League, Mike Long, Jim Mackrell, Tom Merkert, Steve Meyer, Bill Olin, Dave Palmer, Bill Raab, Tom Robinson, Diane Russell, Bob Smith, Steve Smith, Terri Sym, Tom Whiteside, Mary Young, and Stu Young.

Very special thanks to Mary Young. If it weren't for Mary, this project never would have gotten off the ground. She encouraged me to get off my butt, begin organizing my thoughts, and start putting this stuff in writing.

And last thanks to my wife, Jackie, for her patience over the last twelve months as I pursued the above folks for interviews and spent hours and hours in my basement office—which she affectionately refers to as my "cave."

Foreword

Scott and I met in December 1993 at an EMC holiday party when Scott was working for my husband Stu, who was his district manager. From that very first meeting, I knew that Scott Dunkel was a remarkable sales professional and a man with a great love and passion for his job. Over time, Scott and I have become close friends and mentors as we have blazed our respective trails in the competitive landscape of Information technology sales. I have often picked up the phone to ask Scott his advice on topics such as selling to CXO level executives, persuading new sales people to listen to their customers more effectively, building a financial justification in a large complex deal, or helping my career sales people stay fresh and enthusiastic when working in the same accounts year after year. He has always provided valuable insights and direction concerning his time tested approaches to being successful in a professional sales role. Often in these conversations I would say to him, "Scott, you need to write a book. " Thank goodness for all of us," <u>What they don't teach you in sales school</u> ", has become a reality and everyone now can benefit from Scott's experiences and his proven program to deliver breakthrough results.

Today I work for Dell as a Vice President for the Large Enterprise Americas group, responsible for sales and customer satisfaction for Dell's large and upper mid market commercial customers in the eastern United States. This business delivers in excess of $2 billion in annual revenues to Dell from over 1200 corporate customers and employs over 250 first line sales professionals in direct customer support positions. Although I have pursued a path in executive sales management, I have always maintained that the most important element in the success of a large company that derives its revenues from business to business sales is the quality and talent of its first line sales force. Scott is the epitome of the consummate career salesperson. He understands that success is about being a passionate listener and collaborative problem solver. It's about being a customer advocate while being a brand champion for your company and its products. It's about driving big wins and delivering top sales results by focusing on the value of trusted customer relationships built over time.

What makes this book different is Scott's down to earth conversational style and his wealth of solid tips and techniques for success that are time tested and proven. He also includes something you rarely see in a book about professional selling—direct input from high level customer executives so that his readers learn key lessons directly from decision makers. Unlike many books about selling that focus on lofty theories, complex processes, and include countless confusing forms and exercises—Scott focuses on direct, straight forward and no nonsense approaches that he and other top sales professionals he interviewed for this book have used to achieve extraordinary success. Finally, Scott uses real sales stories that are fun to read and act as powerful tools to illustrate the points he is relaying to his audience. His chapters on writing an annual business plan, developing the financial sale, and what to learn from losing a sale are among some of the most impactful reviews of valuable sales techniques I have seen in my 30+ years in business.

All sales professionals should read this book. If you are new to sales and just getting started in this exciting career, this book will show you how to get organized, what are the keys to success, how to set a compass for doing the right things, day after day, so the business will follow. If you are a current sales professional but feel stuck in a rut, unhappy with your current level of success or professional satisfaction, or just trying to "up your game", this book can help you brush up and refocus on the skills and universal truths necessary for sustained top performance. I surely wish I would have had the opportunity to read this book when I started my career as a young IBM sales rep right out of the University of Virginia. I would have saved considerable time and would have prevented some costly errors that, although character building, were avoidable had I learned early the simple truths and strategies that are discussed here.

As I reflect on my long career in the IT industry, I am thrilled with the fact that going into sales and sales management was one of the very best decisions I have ever made. Scott and I have both had the pleasure of watching the products and services we have sold to countless customers enable their growth and drive their success. We have also increased our personal wealth beyond anything we had hoped for while working long hours at a job that we loved so it never felt like work. I know that many of you picking up this book for the first time feel the same way about your decision to go into sales, but may not be as far along in your journey, or may not feel that same sense of accomplishment due to short term challenges that are clouding your way. By embracing the key learnings that Scott so eloquently serves up in this book, you will provide more value to your customers than you could ever imagine while dramatically increasing your own personal job satisfaction and earnings power. In these days of decreased corporate investment in sales training and virtual offices that do not promote face to face coaching, a book like this is more valuable than ever.

Mary C. Young
Vice President, Dell Inc.
Large Enterprise Americas, U.S. East

Introduction

Mark was in elementary school in Southern New Jersey back in 1977 when the teacher went around the room and asked the students what they would like to do when they grew up. The students gave the typical answers youngsters would generally give when asked that question: "I think I'd like to be a doctor or maybe a lawyer." Some said policemen or firemen. When the teacher asked Mark what he wanted to be his answer was a bit different: "I'd like to do what my father does." And he left it like that.

The teacher naturally asked, "Well, what does your father do?"

Mark replied, "To tell you the truth, I really don't know. What I do know is that he's always eating at the best restaurants, plays lots of golf during the week, and works from home quite a bit, and we take family vacations to Vail every year to ski. Whatever he does, I want to do it when I grow up."

Mark's father, Frank, was my sales manager in 1978 when I joined Telex Computer Products. He related this story to us at a sales meeting. You never forget a story like that. While it is funny, there certainly is truth to it. Salespeople do tend to eat in the best restaurants, play a lot of customer golf during the week, and many times work from home. From an outsider's point of view, it does in fact seem like a terrific way to make a living.

However, people tend to focus on the glamorous side of the job and forget what goes on behind the scenes. In other words how did Marks' father get to the point where he could enjoy golfing during the week with clients, nice dinners on the company's expense account, and frequently working from home? Most folks don't start out in an enviable position like this directly out of school. It takes hard work and dedication to the craft of professional selling to reap these benefits. It also helps if you're positioned with the right company with the right product at the right time. These are the areas we will discuss in this book. Just as a professional athlete needs to take steps to be the best he can be, so does a professional sales executive.

In fact there are striking parallels between an NFL quarterback and a professional sales executive. Let's examine some of their attributes in detail.

	NFL Quarterback	Professional Sales Executive
Foundation	Extreme athletic skills, highly coachable, leadership skills, ability to throw every type of pass. Ability to read defenses and know when to run instead of pass.	Outgoing personality, willingness to learn, self-starter, basic sales skills.
System	The right team that will maximize his skill set.	A company with the right product at the right time.
Intangibles	Ability to motivate his team to perform at the highest level. Able to take his team on his back and win the game.	Ability to inspire extreme confidence in his clients and turn a negative situation into a business opportunity.

Just like an NFL quarterback, a person who wants to pursue a career in professional sales must come to the table with a strong *foundation*. Said another way, he should possess some basic characteristics that are fundamental to sales. For example you can't be afraid to pick up the phone and call someone for an appointment. You certainly can't have a fear of rejection. Additionally, you have to be a self-starter and have the ability to work independently, without a lot of supervision. Your foundation should also include basic sales skills such as handling objections, the ability to qualify a prospect, and asking for orders. This is the basic foundation for a successful sales exec, just as the basic foundation for an NFL quarterback is a strong arm and the ability to throw all the necessary deep, medium, and short passes, and to run with the ball on occasion. These are the attributes that allow you to compete at the NFL level or at the highest level in corporate America.

Now, in order to maximize these attributes, you must direct them at the best *system*. We've all seen time and time again quarterbacks who give average performances in one system and flourish in another. Their skill sets haven't changed, but the system in which they're playing has — it's maximizing their potential. This is also true in sales. Your skill set might be a good fit for a particular product or service. That's not to say you couldn't sell another product; you just might not be as successful or enjoy the process as much. A great system has the potential to make a good salesman a great salesman. It's a team effort. And if you're smart enough to take advantage of all the selling resources available, you can be a superstar.

The third attribute is what I refer to as the *intangibles*. Put a great quarterback in a great system that possesses the right intangibles and you have a hall of fame player. He has tremendous leadership skills, knows how to read defenses, can run a two-minute drill and run the ball for a first down when necessary, and win the game when it's on the line. He's taken his game to the highest level and maximized the system in which he plays.

The intangibles, as far as a professional sales exec is concerned, are converting knowledge to wisdom and consistently executing your plan on a daily basis. You learn to maximize the system in which you sell. You don't waste valuable selling time on accounts that offer little or no long-term potential. You learn to focus your energy on the highest potential accounts — the ones that you enjoy working with and that offer the highest potential rewards. After all if you're going to spend a lot of time golfing and dining out, you might as well be doing it with folks you like being around! This is the true definition of mixing business with pleasure.

Additionally, and most importantly, you have the intangible ability to inspire confidence. Your prospects and customers view you as a person of integrity, someone they can count on when problems or issues arise. You are trustworthy, respected, and enjoyable to do business with. You receive opportunities your competitors don't because you are in fact a trusted advisor. You take the sales rep role to the next level.

This book will focus on these intangibles — the final one third of what it takes to escalate you to the highest level of professional sales, the level that will maximize not only your income but your enjoyment. Because if you enjoy your work, there is a good chance you will be more successful.

A sales exec's set of intangibles is, in many cases, the most important ingredient that separates him/her from the pack. The question is: where do you learn these skills? If not from the school of hard knocks then where? Well, you learn from seasoned sales execs and gain valuable wisdom instead of taking many years to learn the same lessons on your own. The purpose of this book is to help professional sales execs who have all the other necessary talents get to this level.

Having said this I truly understand some folks will need to learn these lessons on their own. That's human nature. I was in that category. But those who are willing to listen and learn, and who don't want to go through the pain and suffering I did; will be able to accelerate their sales careers significantly. *Pain and suffering* may be a bit harsh; I truly enjoyed all aspects of my career. However, the fact of the matter is, if I'd had sage advice and LISTENED AND EXECUTED, my career would have accelerated significantly. For whatever reason many of us need to find out for ourselves what works.

In order to gain insight into these intangibles, it was important for me to get input from the three sources that comprise the

"Balancing the stool" chapter of this book: clients, sales management, and sales execs.

Clients-I interviewed several of my former clients as well as other executives who have spent many years interacting with sales folks. The objective was to determine from the buyers' perspective what attributes they like and dislike about sales reps, and how they prefer to be approached and marketed to. In addition I looked at their views on entertainment, proposals, presentations, and negotiations. Conducting these interviews was certainly eye-opening. The stories of how some sales reps have dealt with clients were absolutely stunning. Many of them are related in this book. Hopefully they will serve as a wake-up call.

Sales Management-I spent a significant amount of time interviewing first-line sales managers as well as executive sales management. It's important to get the perspective of the folks who are managing the sales execs. What do they look for when they interview a potential sales exec? How do they manage? How do they prefer to be engaged with clients? What are their views on reports and forecasts? How do they measure productivity other than pure numbers?

Sales Executives-My objective was to interview sales execs who have been successful over the long run. I therefore interviewed those who have been individual contributors for at least twenty years. The logic was if you stayed in direct sales for that long you must have been doing something right. I conducted many interviews in the technology field. I also spoke with several reps in insurance, chemical, lumber broker, and office product businesses as well.

Result-Combining the experience from my thirty-year career in professional sales with that of the three groups I interviewed allowed me to assemble valuable knowledge and wisdom for career-oriented sales folks. The primary objective of this book is to accelerate the learning curve for professional sales execs. The secondary objective is to make it an enjoyable read by relating real sales stories that underscore sales principles. I believe people remember a principle if it is taught through a story that can be applied to their personal sales environments. Additionally, these stories relate to *higher* level principles that I refer to as UNIVERSAL SALES TRUTHS. These are truths that stand the test of time regardless of the timeframe, environment, product, or service. If you adhere to these UNIVERSAL SALES TRUTHS, everything else will take care of itself.

One of my final interviews was with Jim, a career sales exec in the HR software business. Jim had recently taken a position as a sales mentor—a company hired him to offer guidance and support to their sales team. The thought process was they needed some gray hairs to augment the junior reps they were hiring. The sales reps would still report to a traditional sales manager. Jim's role was to provide expertise based on his wisdom and knowledge from a career in sales.

The philosophy of this company was to hire quality folks directly out of college and provide extensive training before releasing them into the field. In fact the training went on for several months. Before graduation each student had to pass a fairly difficult exam and be able to stand up in front of a group and do a PowerPoint presentation on the entire suite of software products they would be selling. Additionally, the employees were trained in traditional sales in terms of cold calling, objection handling, prospecting, negotiating, and how to close business. When they graduated they knew the industry they would be selling to, their products' advantages, the competitive landscape, how to make formal presentations, and basic sales skills. Conventional wisdom would tell you these folks would be ready to take their territories by storm!

Since I was writing this book to help sales people get to the next level, I was very anxious to talk to Jim and get his insight on what areas these junior reps struggled with. His answer took me completely off guard: *"**They don't know what they don't know.**"*

Wow. What was I supposed to do with that information? I wondered. However, the more I spoke with Jim, and the more I thought about it after our meeting, the more sense it made. Companies can't manufacture professional sales execs in a six-month training program. There is no substitute for on-the-job training. Learning product presentations, technical advantages, and how to handle objections does not make a successful sales professional!

In this book I've attempted to cover the *"they don't know what they don't know"* topics. After all if you don't know you're weak in a particular area, how can you get assistance?

WHAT ABOUT A CAREER IN PROFESSIONAL SALES?

When asked the question "what do you want to do when you graduate?" how many people would answer, "I want to spend the rest of my career in sales"? Back up to younger folks and ask the same question. How many would say sales would be their career of choice? Certainly if you just received an MBA a career in sales would be a job of last resort—possibly a way to gain entry into a company, but not something you would consider doing for twenty-five or thirty years. Why is sales typically considered *entry level*? Why don't more folks intentionally make decisions to pursue careers in sales? And why don't people who are successful in sales STAY in sales long term?

I spent almost thirty years in sales. In fact all but two were in direct sales. Yes, I was on quota for nearly three decades . Many folks might think I was either crazy or had little ambition to move up in corporate America. Sales are at the bottom of most organizational charts. The CEO, of course, is at the top. If you're in middle management, pursuing a career in sales would be a move in the wrong direction, at least in terms of the org chart. Based on commissions and bonuses, many people in sales can earn far more than most employees at even the highest levels in many companies.

But still salespeople are typically not considered executive-level employees. They are simply sales reps. We give them all kinds or interesting titles designed to pump them up and maybe give prospects the feeling that they're being called on by a high-level person. I went back and looked at as many old business cards as I could find just to see my titles. Remember, I was simply a sales rep with *no* management responsibility. Here is a sample of my titles:

Account representative
Senior account representative
Major account representative
District sales manager
Territory manager
Account executive
Senior account manager

Bottom line, your company — or you — can call it anything you want but the fact of the matter is you are a **sales rep**. One of the reasons I've written this book is to share the simple fact that this is **OK**. Whether you're a sales rep for a short amount of time or for a career, it is a tremendous learning experience that should be valued and not taken lightly. In what other profession do you have the opportunity to meet, negotiate with, and socialize with executives who are, in most cases, many years your senior? In what profession do you have the opportunity to earn more than the executives you are calling on? In what profession do you have the opportunity to influence the direction of the products or services you represent without being an insider or at the executive level? Most importantly, sales execs are primarily responsible for top-line revenue growth. It is for these reasons that professional salespeople should be regarded as the most important ingredients in a company's org chart. At least that's my opinion—but I am somewhat biased.

I'll never forget a comment one of my professors at St. John's University in New York made in the fall of 1972. It was my freshman year, and I was trying to determine what my major would be within the school of business. As I recall the choices were as follows:

Accounting
Finance
Management
Marketing

The professor said something like, "You could have the best mousetrap on the planet, but if no one knows about it, it will never sell!"

Think about that for a moment. We've all bought products because of outstanding marketing and sales campaigns. After purchasing the products, they've disappointed us or flat-out didn't work as advertised. On the other hand, some products are well-kept secrets. Because of a lack of marketing or sales activities, they never make it and die slow deaths.

In any event the professor's statement stuck in my head, and I decided to major in marketing. As a freshman at St. John's I honestly felt that getting a degree in marketing would most likely prepare me for a long career in the marketing department of a major corporation. Maybe I would help design a campaign for Proctor & Gamble or General Motors. Perhaps I would start as a junior executive and work my way up the ladder to VP of worldwide marketing. In all honesty this was how I thought back in 1972.

So after graduation in 1976, I began looking for my first job in the field of marketing. It didn't take long to figure out that there weren't any! The next best thing to pursue was an entry-level position as a sales rep. After all once I proved myself in sales I would be able to move up to marketing. At least this was the message I was getting on interviews.

The company I really wanted to work for was IBM. It was viewed in the marketplace as having the best development programs for young executives and certainly was a well-respected company with many benefits. I would start in sales and then other opportunities would open up. There was, however, one small problem: they didn't view Scott Dunkel as IBM material. You see they had very high standards, and I apparently didn't meet them. Ultimately I interviewed with the Burroughs Corporation, a competitor of IBM, and began my career in sales in the spring of 1976. I'm a firm believer that things happen for a reason, and not working for IBM turned out to be in my best interest in the long run. My entire career was based on selling *against* IBM. Like an undrafted free agent who's looking for a shot at the NFL, many times you work harder because of the chip on your shoulder. You want to prove the naysayers wrong and excel at your craft.

I started my career in direct sales and ended my career in direct sales. This was not a well thought out strategy that I'm attempting to take credit for. It is, however, one of the reasons I've written this book—because looking back, it should have been. It is my hope that folks who enjoy the challenge of direct sales might rethink their career options and consider staying in the field. Based on my story as well as many others described in this book, professional sales rep can be an awesome career. It does *not* have to be a stepping-stone to bigger and better opportunities. It can be the final stop if executed properly.

Take a look at the Professional Sales Cycle Pyramid on the following page. It covers all the necessary steps, from uncovering a prospect to bringing it to closure. Additionally, it highlights all the attributes a sales executive must possess to be successful long term. Once a sale is finally made, it becomes necessary to switch from being a sales rep to being more of an account manager. These are two distinct skill sets. However, a true professional will excel in both. In my career I have witnessed terrific sales reps who lacked account management skills. I have also witnessed tremendous account reps who had no clue how to sell a new account.

The bottom line is a professional sales executive needs to learn a variety of skills in order to be successful long term. Smart companies truly value and make every effort to retain these high-level performers. If you are one of them, a career in professional sales will not only be rewarding but also provide tremendous job security for you and your family.

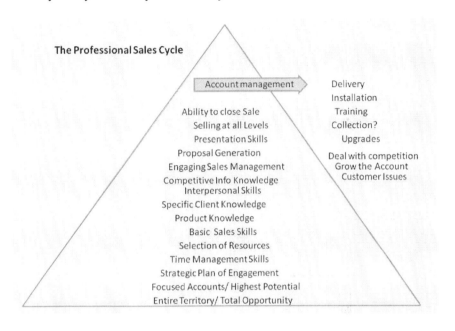

The Professional Sales Cycle

Account management

Delivery
Installation
Training
Collection?
Upgrades

Deal with competition
Grow the Account
Customer Issues

Ability to close Sale
Selling at all Levels
Presentation Skills
Proposal Generation
Engaging Sales Management
Competitive Info Knowledge
Interpersonal Skills
Specific Client Knowledge
Product Knowledge
Basic Sales Skills
Selection of Resources
Time Management Skills
Strategic Plan of Engagement
Focused Accounts/ Highest Potential
Entire Territory/ Total Opportunity

HOW TO UTILIZE THIS BOOK BEST

In each chapter of this book, I have attempted to relate a high-level sales principle to a real-life sales situation from my career or another seasoned sales exec. Additionally, based on interviews with sales managers and clients, I have compiled a whole host of stories that drive home particular sales principles. Receiving input from senior executives who deal with professional sales execs on a daily basis was very insightful. I recommend that as you read these stories you put the book down for a moment now and then and reflect on the stories and principles. Think about how the truth I've related can be applied to your sales activities. It is my belief that people will remember facts and principles if they are born of a real-life story. And if the story is entertaining or funny, there is a better chance it will be remembered as well. It is my hope that these universal truths of selling will become important components of the way you approach your clients.

Over the last year, I interviewed key decision makers at the executive level. I also spoke with executive sales management to get their perspective on what it takes to perform at the highest level and what attributes they deem necessary for success. Finally I interviewed successful sales execs who spent the lions' shares of their careers as individual contributors. So the bottom line is I got valuable input from *all* sides of the sales triangle: the sales rep, sales management, and the client. Based on all of these interviews in conjunction with my thirty-year career in sales, I documented the key ingredients that, if executed on a continuing basis, will result in long-term success.

This book is designed to get you to THINK! Apply the stories and principles you find here to your individual situation. They certainly will not all be exact matches, but they should resonate with you if you take the time to reflect.

You might be wondering what I mean by UNIVERSAL SALES TRUTHS. These are constant regardless of what you're selling or the timeframe in which you live and work. In other words whether you were selling sheep 500 years ago or specialized software in 2012, these universal truths remain constant. People are people and prefer to be treated with respect and dignity. This is an example of a truth that certainly will stand the test of time. It is also a truth that applies not only to sales but to your personal interactions with people in general.

This book will attempt to move you from knowledge to wisdom. Knowledge is certainly good and helpful. However, if it is not applied effectively it is useless. There is a big difference between having the facts and applying them! For example you might know that eating healthy and putting yourself on a strict exercise regimen is good for your overall health. However, your busy schedule and the fact that you're always eating in restaurants makes this knowledge not particularly useful. It is the application of knowledge that makes the difference. We should do our best to live out what we know.

The principles in this book apply to the sales exec who is willing to make a commitment to the craft of selling for the long term. It is not a "how to make a quick buck in sales" book. Professional sales are a marathon, not a sprint. Applying these universal truths of selling will pay dividends over an extended period of time. That might mean you'll lose a deal or two along the way because you refuse to compromise your integrity for a one-off transaction.

These universal truths are timeless, and if adhered to completely can simplify the way you approach selling. They can be traced back to Solomon, who many people believe was the wisest man to walk the face of the earth. Solomon wrote literally hundreds of proverbs. I've identified fifteen that specifically relate to professional sales. Unfortunately for me I learned these universal truths in the school of hard knocks. It was only a few years ago that I uncovered them in written form. If they had been introduced to me earlier in life, I could have accelerated my selling success and avoided much stress.

I encourage you to read these universal truths. They are located in the back of the book. They are all very short and to the point. You can read them in less than five minutes.

THE SALES TRIANGLE WITH ONE IMPORTANT ADDITION

The chart below has only one addition. However, it is the most important ingredient: the foundation! Even if you have mastered all of the components of the sales triangle, without a strong foundation you will never reach your maximum potential. It is akin to building a beautiful home on a wood foundation—it will not withstand the test of time.

The universal sales truths that serve as the foundation are fundamental to all components of the sales triangle. I touch on these truths in every chapter of this book. In my opinion they should guide every aspect of your business life.

Did you ever wonder why you lost a major order? You had the best solution as well as a competitive price, yet another company with an inferior offering won the business. There is a strong chance you lost because you did not adhere to all of the universal sales truths. It all starts with a strong *foundation*.

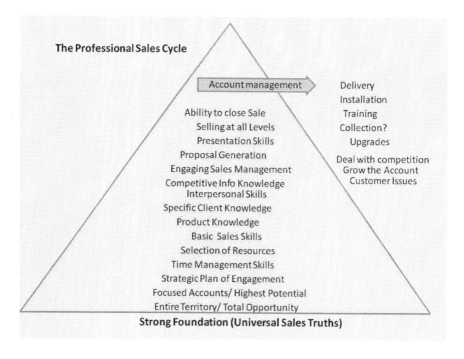

CHAPTER 1

DEVELOPING YOUR ANNUAL BUSINESS PLAN

The first step for anyone starting a new business is to prepare a detailed business plan. Why is that? Because as the saying goes, if you fail to plan you are planning to fail! The fact of the matter is YOU are running a small business. Your territory is your marketplace, and it is your responsibility to maximize the revenue potential as best you can. Running your territory is very similar to running a small business. That's why I said early on in this book that the skills you develop over a career in sales position you quite effectively to run a small business. The major difference is that in a small business you use your money. While working in corporate America, you use your employer's money.

As a small business owner you strive to maximize revenues and minimize expenses. At the end of the year you will produce a profit-and-loss statement that will reflect the success of your business. Similarly, as a professional sales executive, you will be evaluated on your revenue generation. In some companies your annual expenses will be taken into consideration as well. After all expenses are a key component of the net profit of the

1

company you represent. Some companies have very generous expense account policies, and some are just the opposite. Keep in mind that any out-of-pocket business expenses you incur are tax deductable. That, of course, is for expenses for which your company does not reimburse you.

A small business's initial plan will require a lot more research and time than the follow-on annual updates. This is typically true for a salesman entering a new territory with a new product as well. Let's take a look at the components of a business plan from a new salesman's perspective—let's call him Harry. For the purpose of this discussion, we will assume Harry is representing a new product in a new geographic territory of several states, and his annual quota is $800,000. His company offers a $1,000 bonus for opening up a new account, and the commission rate is 5 percent.

Harry has set a personal goal of earning $100,000. We will also assume he has no existing relationships with any accounts in his new territory. The bottom line he is starting from ground zero. The good news is he has been in sales for five years, selling a competitive product in the same industry. He will ramp up quickly in terms of product knowledge and feels very comfortable representing this new product. His biggest challenge is to determine how and where he should spend his time in order to reach his income objective.

In such a case, the biggest challenge is to attain as much valuable information about his new territory as possible. Here are a few suggestions:

Former sales executives-Do your best to track down the sales folks who have called on the accounts in your territory. This is the best source of information. Buy them lunch or dinner, and learn as much as you can about their success or lack of. Don't allow them to discourage you in any way. Listen and take notes. Ask if they can send you their contact lists with telephone numbers and e-mail addresses. If you are fortunate your company may have required the former salespeople to document all information relative to each account in the territory. Software tools like salesforce.com or ACT would provide you with very specific and detailed information on the activity in your new territory as well.

Sales managers-Hopefully your sales manager has some experience with the accounts in your territory. Get as much detail as possible as well as his list of contacts. Compare his views of the accounts with the former sales reps and begin to formulate your own opinion about the account base.

Office administrators-Many times office admin folks have worked with the accounts in your territory through the years. Set up a time to meet with them and learn as much as you can. Again, ask for their contact lists.

Support Personnel-Depending on the nature of your product or service offering, there may be people in your office who have spent time at accounts in your territory. For example if you're selling copiers or some other office equipment, technicians who have serviced your accounts may have valuable information that will help you. Don't forget to get their contact lists as well.

Company files-You might be surprised at what you find in old file cabinets. Check your office files for information on your account base. You might find interesting information that pre-dates any of the folks you have met with.

Previous customers-If you have been in the industry for a while, go through your list of contacts to see if any of your previous business contacts know anyone in your new territory.

Industry data-Many times you can purchase lists that provide information on the accounts in your territory. For example in the IT business a company called IDC (International Data Corp) offer a valuable database with information such as the size of the data center, the chief information officer, technical contacts, and growth plans. In some cases the information may not be up to date. It does, however, offer a solid starting point and certainly gives a genuine sense of the size of the account. You can also do your own research on the Internet or at a library. Social media such as LinkedIn or Facebook might offer accurate contact data as well.

Current client Files-Hopefully your territory includes some existing clients. Spend time reviewing the files so you can understand the histories and buying patterns of your new customers.

These are eight potential resources to deploy in order to glean valuable information relative to your new territory. I suggest opening a file folder for each and every account. Continue to update it as you use these resources in order to build a solid account base. As you begin to call on these accounts, you will obviously update each folder with your own information. However, for the purpose of this discussion, we are using this data in order to determine where we should focus our time and energy. This is the starting point of our business plan.

Let's assume Harry did this research on his territory and came up with the following information. Remember these are accounts that have needs for your product or service.

- Two hundred total accounts
- Eighty small accounts
- Twenty very large accounts (one is a customer)
- One hundred medium-size accounts
- Ten current customers

From this overall account breakdown, Harry can begin to put his plan in place for how he can achieve his income objective of $100,000. He has to decide where to focus his time and energy in order to generate enough sales to meet his objective.

Through discussion with his manager and other sales reps, he determines the typical medium-size account does an average of $50K per year in business. The small accounts do less than $10K per year, and the very large accounts do an average of $100K. He also knows some very large accounts can do more than $200K on occasion.

So Harry now knows the overall potential business in his territory — that is if his company receives *all* the business. We know this is impossible. Even if Harry is a superstar salesperson, he will not get all the business. From a big-picture perspective, he begins to put his high-level plan in place. Harry determines he needs to do business with about twelve medium-size accounts and two very large accounts in order to reach his quota of $800K.

12 x $50K= $600K
2 x $100K =$200K
Total sales ($800K) at 5% = $40K in commission

Additionally, he feels confident he can sell at least ten new accounts. The compensation plan offers a $1,000 bonus for every new account. This will generate an additional $10K in compensation. He therefore summarizes his annual plan like this:

Salary: $50K
Commission: $40K
Bonus: $10K
Forecasted income: $100K

Harry has now completed the first part of his business plan. He has identified the accounts in his territory. He has also broken it down by revenue potential. Finally he has applied his income objective to his territory in order to forecast how many accounts he needs to do business with to achieve his income goal.

Now is the time to drill down into this account base in more detail. Let's look at each account in six critical areas:

- **Geography**
- **Revenue potential**
- **Competitive landscape**
- **Current clients**
- **History and background**
- **Ability to pay**

Geography-Depending on the size of your territory, geography can play an important role in your territory analysis. However, regardless of your territory size, I believe it is helpful to categorize your customers and prospects by geography. This will allow you to be efficient with your time, which is your most valuable asset. Don't waste it by driving from one part of your territory to other. Be smart about how you arrange your appointments so as to maximize your time in front of clients.

Generally speaking, the more quality calls you make the more success you will have. This comes from solid planning. Additionally, if you have a very large geography that requires airplane travel, you absolutely want to call on as many accounts as you can in one trip. This goes without saying but does require lots of advance planning. The fact is you may have five accounts in a remote part of your territory that requires either a six-hour drive or a short flight. Unless these five accounts offer reasonable potential, it may be in your best interest to put them on the back burner. This, of course, depends on the potential in other parts of your territory. This is why territory analysis and solid planning are critical.

At the end of this exercise you will have grouped your accounts by geography, and you will have your file folders cat-egorized by geography as well. In my case I had a folder each for Baltimore, DC, Northern Virginia, Eastern Shore, etc.

Revenue potential-This reflects the overall revenue potential of each account in your territory. This is what each account is capable of purchasing in total on an annual basis. As we will see shortly, this metric might not be the deciding factor regarding the *real* opportunity for your company. It simply reflects the overall potential of the prospect or customer.

Competitive landscape-This metric might be the most difficult to quantify. What you're attempting to determine is the difficulty in doing business with this account. The landscape takes into con-sideration many factors. First and foremost you need to determine your *competitive advantage*. If you can't identify why a prospect should do business with you, then it will be difficult to gain a foot-hold in the account. When you call the account for an appointment, what reason to meet will you give? You had better be prepared to understand what competing products your prospect has installed and why the account should spend time with you. To be effective you would need to research how your product or service will solve your prospect's problem better than their current supplier.

As an example, when I worked for EMC Corporation in the mid 1990s, we had a data storage system that outperformed the IBM product offering. However, if the client did not have a performance issue, then they might not see the value in changing suppliers. It was my responsibility as a professional to take the time to understand the client's environment — specifically to learn which applications were mission-critical to the organization. I knew if I could improve the performance of a critical application that generated revenue and profits, I had a much better chance of success.

So that's exactly what I did. My technical team spent time understanding where the pain was and forecasted the difference in processing time if EMC storage were deployed. We then installed an evaluation system to confirm our analysis. If we didn't meet the performance improvement we forecasted, then the client did not have to accept the system. It was a win-win situation for EMC and the prospect.

Getting back to the competitive landscape metric, if you have a "me too" product with no discernible advantage, then you might be selling on price, delivery, or service. That's fine as long as you can articulate the value and your prospect agrees. The message is: make sure you are confident you can offer your prospect a valuable alternative to his current supplier. If you honestly can't, then I would submit you don't have a viable prospect. Go find someone else to call on!

Current clients-First and foremost let me say that the first place you should fully understand is your current installed base. As you're evaluating the rest of your territory, you should immediately make calls on *all* of the installed clients therein. This is regardless of what other folks have told you about the accounts. I've seen numerous situations where new sales folks were told not to waste any time with account XYZ. While it is good to seek advice, as I said earlier, it is up to you to make the final decision regarding where you spend your time. I have seen other situations where the client and the previous sales rep did not see eye to eye — they flat-out did not get along, and therefore business was lost. In any event it is up to you to call on the account and make every attempt to make a fresh start. Many times the client will welcome you and offer you a legitimate opportunity to earn their business. You will only know for sure if you give it a chance. This, of course, is an extreme case.

Let's assume the account you're inheriting is a happy customer. This is the optimal situation, and it is your responsibility to make sure the account continues to be happy. You therefore would spend quality time with the key decision maker and learn firsthand why they like doing business with your company. Then you will do your best to make sure your company continues to provide the products and services your client has come to expect.

Ask the right questions and learn from a happy customer. This information not only will help you keep this client happy but will also help you understand why other prospects will enjoy doing business with you. This client will be a key asset in terms of reference selling for you.

Additionally, and probably most importantly, an existing client should be the easiest source of revenue for you in the upcoming year. You would expect to have a better chance of closing business in a current account than in a brand new one. Customers that are happy typically don't go out of their way to change vendors. Treat *all* of your current accounts with respect and dignity. They are the most valuable assets in your new territory. Never lose sight of this!

Having said this it is also important to mention that all accounts, existing as well as new, always need to be evaluated in terms of the traditional cost/benefit analysis. What I mean by this is if an account occupies more of your time than the return generated, you need to fire that account! Simply put if an account takes up a tremendous amount of your selling time or your support staff's time, you should evaluate whether or not the account is worth keeping. This may seem counterintuitive, but the fact of the matter is you have a limited amount of time in your workweek. How you spend it determines your success.

Additionally, some accounts can become emotionally draining. They continually beat you up over trivial matters and are always looking for discounts or some reason to pay you less.

You know the type. You cringe every time you see their guy's number on your cell phone. It sucks the wind out of you and impacts your ability to be upbeat on your next sales call. If this persists and the revenue generated is fairly insignificant then I would encourage you to fire this client. Not in a nasty way, but simply tell them it's obvious to you that your company can't provide the service they're demanding, so you encourage them to look elsewhere. This might be one of the most enjoyable meetings you ever have. It will also serve notice that you are nobody's punching bag and you can live without the business this client provides. This might call the account's bluff, and their attitude in future dealings might change. Regardless of the outcome, you must guard your time and use it effectively. If this client is your largest, then the decision will be much harder.

To summarize, take the necessary time to understand the landscape of your existing client base. Find out what they like and dislike about doing business with your company. Then put an action plan together to secure their business.

History and background-This is a broad topic. What I mean by *history and background* are all of the intangible components that make up your prospect. It includes their past buying habits, their corporate culture, their management team, what companies they traditionally do business with, and whether they focus on price, quality, or service. By doing proper research in this broad area, you will come up with a gut feel for your opportunity to do business with this prospect.

As an example if you find out that the son-in-law of the buying contact at your prospect is your competitor, then there is a strong likelihood it will be difficult to do business with this client. Or if you determine that all acquisitions at your prospect go to the purchasing department for final approval, and you know you're not the lowest-price supplier, then the chances are minimal you will win the business. In my case, back in the late '70s, I found out through a technical contact within Con Edison that senior management only bought from IBM. But instead of packing my bags and finding another prospect to sell to, I continued to spend valuable time at the account. Let me explain:

I had worked hard to install a demo 3270 display at Con Edison in New York City. For those of you who don't know, Con Edison is the electric and gas supplier in the New York metropolitan area. They were a very large IBM mainframe account and therefore represented significant potential for my 3270 alternative products. Remember, I represented Telex Computer Products; they manufactured display terminals and printers that attached directly to IBM mainframe computers. They were functionally equivalent and offered some technical advantages but were not manufactured by IBM.

After several months of navigating the landscape I found the technical contact that was responsible for evaluating and recommending to senior management what products to purchase. His name was Frank, and I developed a close working relationship with him. I had installed several products for evaluation. Frank informed me he found Telex products very favorable and he would recommend them to senior management. Needless to say I was very excited about the prospect of doing business with Con Ed. They were one of my largest potential accounts.

Then Frank told me something in confidence. He was very frustrated as he related this to me. He said he had recommended alternative products to IBM to senior management on many occasions. The result was always the same: they continued to purchase IBM products regardless of his recommendations. In fact, he said, they would probably purchase paper from IBM if they could. He gave me the impression that there was some political connection at a very high level that created this situation. Without coming out and saying it he basically felt his job as an evaluator was a big waste of time.

After learning this information, any respectable salesperson would have removed his demo equipment and moved on. That is not what Scott Dunkel did. I felt compelled to help Frank change the current reality of purchasing at Con Ed. So, at the tender age of twenty-five, I sent a letter to the senior vice president in charge of information technology, articulating Frank's frustration in great detail. What's funny is I honestly felt I was doing Frank a favor, and Telex would finally be doing business with Con Ed.

What happened next was very interesting. I received a call from the SVP's admin, requesting a meeting with me and my manager, Bill. When we arrived for the meeting, we were escorted to the SVP's office. His name was Joseph. He was probably in his late fifties and was dressed impeccably — he looked the part of a senior executive. And his office was huge! I had never been in an office of that size. His desk was at one side of the room, and the sofa Bill and I sat on was at the other, as far as possible from the desk, which was up on a platform so Joe was looking down at us. It would have been helpful to have binoculars to see him. By the way, my technical contact, Frank, was in the room as well.

As you can imagine, Joe had not called us in to give us our first order. What he did was make it clear that Con Ed did in fact purchase products from companies other than IBM. He was extremely unhappy about my letter, which inferred there was no opportunity for anyone but IBM. His tone was very serious, and it was clear he was annoyed that he'd had to take time from his busy schedule to meet with us. He then asked Frank to explain the many products they bought that were not from IBM.

Frank looked like a small child who had just been reprimanded by his teacher. He seemed to have trouble speaking. Joseph was probably five or six levels above him in the management chain. This may have been the first time Frank was in Joseph's office and the first time they'd been in a meeting together. Frank struggled to come up with a few purchases Con Ed made that were non-IBM. I felt horrible for having put him in this situation. He had trusted me with information, and I'd had no business using it as I'd done.

The meeting did not last very long. Joseph had made his point. The buying habits of Con Ed were not going to change. All I'd done was waste valuable selling time, and more importantly put Frank in a precarious position with senior management. This was a valuable lesson to learn. Don't do as I did!

Ability to pay-Sounds basic, doesn't it? Yet many times, in our haste to do business, we lose sight of this fact. Many companies have credit or accounts receivable departments that require credit checks, bank statements, references, etc. before equipment is shipped or services are rendered. That's all well and fine. But that doesn't do you much good after you've spent a significant amount of selling time with this prospect. Let's say for example you spent the better part of a year working a major opportunity at company XYZ. You've spent your company's money on entertainment. You've even spent some of your own money. Additionally, you've deployed significant company resources in terms of bringing in other folks to support your efforts. You've been awarded your first contract and expect significant follow-on business. The corporate lawyers from your company and your new client are hammering out the details of the master agreement.

The very last step in the process is the mundane task of checking your new client's credit. Then it happens: your credit manager will not ship unless the client agrees to pay COD. It seems they have a history of being a late pay. And your company will not extend credit. You are devastated! Your primary sales contact wants your product, but he has no control over the payables department, who refuses to do business on a COD basis. You go back to your credit manager, and he refuses to ship and extend credit.

You're at an impasse. You've gotten your deal to the one-foot line on the proverbial football field and you can't punch it in. This dilemma could have been avoided with a little bit of upfront homework. Take the time to have your company do its due diligence in terms of credit checks early on in your sales campaign. Get this all behind you before you spend a lot of your valuable time. And if it turns out the potential client does in fact have bad credit, you have the opportunity to discuss COD with your prospect far in advance of contract time. Maybe there are alternatives to explore. Maybe you can sell to a finance company that can resell to your client at a profit. The bottom line is you want to address this issue early, not at the last minute.

I've mixed in some sales strategies and best practices in this chapter because I feel it's important to address them while discussing how you segment your account base. Obviously, when preparing your annual business plan, you won't be doing credit checks on your prospects. It is, however, an important component of your ability to do business with a particular account. At some point it will be necessary.

Now you have segregated your entire territory by *geography, revenue potential, competitive landscape, current clients, history and background, and ability to pay.* This data can be on a computer or in file folders or both. Either way you'll have a true picture of your TOTAL sales potential. And if you have done your job right, you will have a good feel for which accounts offer the best low-hanging fruit — in other words what accounts will offer immediate revenue potential.

Your database will help you to become more efficient because it will be broken out by geography as well, so you can make good use of your time. Using all of the above metrics, you will rank the accounts in terms of priority. This way you will maximize your valuable time with the highest-potential accounts. This is critical because you don't want to give equal time to all accounts. You want to give more time to high-potential, likely-to-purchase-from-you accounts and minimal time to low-potential, unlikely-to-purchase-from-you accounts. This, of course, is an oversimplification, but I trust you get my point.

If you remember, we assumed Harry had a total of two hundred accounts in his territory. There was a mix of small, medium, and very large accounts. Additionally, there were ten current customers. After Harry analyzed his territory, he determined that in order to have the best chance of hitting his quota and earning his target income he would focus as follows:

- Fifteen very large accounts (out of a total of twenty)
- Twenty small accounts (out of a total of eighty)
- Fifty medium accounts (out of a total of one hundred)
- Eight current accounts (out of a total of ten)

Harry felt if he focused on these ninety-three accounts he would hit his targets. He was somewhat concerned that he would not focus on the other 107 accounts in his territory. But he realized he had limited time in his workweek and wanted to be as productive as possible. It didn't mean he completely forgot about the other 107 accounts; it simply meant he would not *focus* on them. In other words he would put very specific strategies in place for his ninety-three target accounts. The remaining accounts he would contact, and perhaps make a sales call or two to confirm his suspicions. If he uncovered information during these cursory calls that indicated potential he didn't foresee, then of course he would reevaluate his initial decision.

With some of the 107 accounts he might not even have made personal sales calls. Harry might have made phone or e-mail inquiries. It all gets back to time management. Speaking from experience it is very difficult not to make a concerted effort to sell to everyone in your territory. But the fact of the matter is you don't have the time to put a quality sales campaign together for all of your accounts. So you're forced to make a decision; take the necessary time to make it the correct one. Your objective is to focus on the accounts that are most likely to do business with your company and that represent the highest potential.

Perhaps the most difficult part of your annual business plan is now complete: you've identified the accounts you plan to focus on this year. Now the planning process begins. Your plan or strategy to do business at these target accounts will be comprised of some or all of these components:

- Determining the economic buyer/final decision maker
- Understanding who is the primary recommender
- Determining how to connect with the client
- Use of entertainment
- Competitive landscape
- Your primary competitive advantage
- Sales manager/senior level involvement
- Deployment of necessary resources
- Corporate culture
- Proposal generation

During this phase of your business plan, you lay out the specific strategy to nurture your account from prospect to valued client. The above components are merely a starting point. It is up to you as the sales professional to determine what is needed and how much time you will spend. Remember, time is your most valuable resource. Plan your strategy and execute it. If it turns out that you're spending way too much time on a particular account without any progress, you may be well served to modify your plan accordingly.

Again, the purpose of this chapter is to help you outline the components of a sales business plan. You are now very close to completion. The final phase is to place a dollar value on each of the accounts you will be focusing on. In Harry's example if he had ninety-three targeted accounts in his plan he would not have the time to prepare a detailed strategy for each. He might, however, have put a detailed plan together for the very large potential accounts and done an abbreviated plan for the medium and small accounts. Regardless, he would forecast a revenue target for each of these accounts. Remember, his annual revenue objective was $800K. Naturally his plan should have totaled at least this amount—hopefully even more!

In the event you do your due diligence and honestly feel your targeted accounts do not add up to your annual quota, then you will have a strong argument for a reduction in quota. The last thing good sales managers want is to assign quotas that are unattainable. If, in fact, by virtue of a solid and well thought out business plan, you show it will be impossible to achieve your quota, then all the work you did upfront will have paid off. If the quota remains the same, at least you have gone on record with management and will be in a good position next year to receive a reduction.

To summarize, your annual business plan will have a list of accounts, a forecasted revenue target, and a brief description of the strategy to gain the business. This is your roadmap for the upcoming year. It will most likely change. However, it is critical that you have this starting point. As you progress through the calendar year, you will update the document. Specifically you will attach sales figures to your target accounts and sales figures to your non-targeted accounts. Additionally you will modify the focus based on circumstances that present themselves.

As time goes on, your annual business plan becomes a living document that tracks your progress. At the end of the year it will be interesting to see how accurate you were. Hopefully the longer you are in the territory the more accurate you will be able to forecast your business by individual account.

Incidentally, many companies require their sales folks to prepare plans like this on an annual basis. Regardless, this is something you *should* do. No need to be asked. This will benefit you and serve as a platform for discussion when meeting with sales management. If done properly it will set you apart from the other sales folks in the office.

CHAPTER REVIEW

- Use all necessary resources to understand the total potential of your territory.
- Focus on the accounts that will provide the best opportunities to meet your objectives.
- Put a solid plan in place for each of your focused accounts.
- Adjust your annual plan accordingly as the year unfolds.

CHAPTER 2

HOW WELL DO YOU KNOW YOUR PRODUCT OR SERVICE?

W hen making a sales call, few things inspire more confidence than a deep understanding of your product or service. In my career there were several occasions where I couldn't answer questions I should have been able to. In those cases I was completely honest and told my prospects I would get back to them ASAP with the answers. I would not advocate guessing or making something up.

However, when a prospect asks several questions and you are constantly telling them you will get back to them, it doesn't inspire confidence. If you represent a very technical product and you are calling on a technical individual, then you obviously need to have assistance. In my case at Memorex/Telex or EMC, we had systems engineers available who could speak the language of the technical folks at our accounts. Alternatively we could bring in resources from out of town. I would very rarely make a sales call on a technical individual without backup.

However, it's up to you to know your audience. The purpose of this chapter is to review the types of questions you should, as a professional, be able to articulate without calling for help.

Back in the early '80s, I was calling on Greater SE Community Hospital in Washington, DC. I had a 3270-compatible terminal on evaluation at the time. Before I would bring one in for a trial I would always ask what the display would be used for. In this particular case, Rich, the DP manager, said they would be doing lots of numeric inputs. We had several keyboard choices available, and one had a numeric keypad. I naturally shipped this one in for the evaluation.

After about a week, I stopped back to meet with Rich to discuss the progress of the evaluation. He said everyone who tried our device liked it. The display was clear, and it worked, from a technical standpoint, identical to the IBM product .Then he said something I never forgot: the operators really liked the numeric pad on the keyboard. They said it improved their productivity since it was set up exactly like an adding machine. Then he went on to say IBM did not offer a numeric keypad. At that point I was shocked because I knew IBM did in fact offer a numeric keypad. I was about to tell Rich, "Yeah, what a shame IBM doesn't offer that option." Then, in a split second, I made the decision to tell him the truth. I asked Rich who told him IBM didn't offer a numeric keypad. He responded that it was his IBM sales rep. Think about it: I knew more about the IBM product than the IBM rep. I took a chance by telling the truth, but I had a sneaking suspicion Rich would appreciate the honesty and prefer to do business with a rep who knew his product and was working for the business. Greater SE Community turned into a nice account for Telex.

In this chapter we will discuss the importance of knowing your product or service, which goes way beyond the technical details of your offering. For example if I walked into a major IBM computer installation and started talking to the CIO about the technical capabilities of my product and why it was better than his current supplier, I would not have stood a chance of doing business. Even if the product worked and was less expensive, most executives are not willing to take chances without doing their due diligence and complete evaluations. When investing hundreds of thousands of dollars on mission-critical systems, decisions are not taken lightly.

So when I talk about knowing your product or service, I am speaking about *all* the necessary components of that product or service. These go far beyond the technical capabilities of the offering. Let's take a look at some of them, though keep in mind that in your particular industry there may be others.

Beyond the product or service, it is important to understand what you need to do in order to make your prospect comfortable with you, your company, and your product. Many sales folks don't understand why they lose business. They might say something like, "We had a much better technical solution and a competitive price. I can't understand how we lost the deal."

In some cases the simple answer is you failed to connect with your prospect. We will spend quite a bit of time on this important topic. After all if you fail to make a connection with your prospect you are fighting an uphill battle.

Here are a few areas to consider:

- The company you represent
- The industry you are selling to
- Your track record
- References
- Market share
- Service and support
- Your experience
- Your product relative to the competition

Let's look at each of these individually. Depending on the product or service you represent, they may or may not be relevant.

The company you represent-If you represent a company with products or services that are an important ingredient of the success of your prospect, then your company is very important. Clients want to feel comfortable with the company as well as the product. They want to be sure the company will be around long term. What's the point of establishing a relationship with a company that is on shaky financial ground and might not be around to support the sale? Or maybe it's the target of a takeover by a larger company, which means the support after the sale could be different.

It's your responsibility to position the company you represent in a positive light. To do this you must know certain key points. For example how long has it been in business? Is it public or private? If it's public how has the stock performed over the last several years? Additionally, you should know some basic financial information on your company. When I represented EMC, for example, I emphasized the financial strength of the company as well as its stock performance. This was a major competitive advantage over some of the smaller startup companies that were attempting to compete against us. Conversely, when I represented Memorex/ Telex, the financial aspect was not an advantage and in fact presented a major challenge at times. I did attempt to paint a positive outlook as best I could without being untruthful.

The industry you are selling to-It has been my experience that prospects like to know that other folks in their industry are using the same product or service. For example when I represented Telex Computer Products back in the early '80s I focused a lot of my selling efforts on hospitals. We offered a light pen option that allowed a nurse to order medicine and supplies by touching it to a display screen.

I also made it a point to leverage the relationships and experiences from one hospital to another. What you find is that both executives and technical folks tend to move around within the same industry. As a professional sales executive, this can be a tremendous business advantage. When a happy client from one hospital lands at another hospital where you currently don't have a presence, it provides an instant opportunity. From my perspective, when calling a new hospital prospect it was nice to be able to mention ten other hospitals in the Baltimore/Washington area that were currently using our display terminals. Typically my prospect would ask me if I knew so and so at one of the hospitals I mentioned. This would help establish an immediate connection as well as a level of comfort with me and my company.

To a lesser degree I used the same approach in the banking and insurance industries as well as state and local government.

You will find that the more you become a specialist in a particular industry the easier it is to do business. Clients prefer dealing with sales folks who understand the challenges of their industry as opposed to a sales rep who is more of a generalist.

Your track record-This can be a very touchy subject, but rest assured a potential client will be interested in learning about your company's track record. This is basically your report card over a period of time. For example if you were to select a mutual fund for your investment portfolio you would look at its track record.

We all know past performance is no guarantee of future performance, but this is all we have to go on. If you play the horses, pretty much the only way to handicap the race is by looking at past performances. So your prospect will ask questions about your track record. Be prepared to give several examples of how you and your company have responded to your clients' needs. These examples should roll off your tongue and inspire confidence in your prospect. The track record involves all of the components of servicing your accounts from the time the order is taken to the time it is delivered as well as the ongoing support.

References-This, in my opinion, is one of the most important components of knowing your product or service. For me reference selling was the easiest way to soft sell my prospects. Why? Because if it's done correctly, your reference does most of the selling.

When I speak of reference selling I'm not saying simply to give your prospect a sheet of paper with five names and phone numbers on it. That is *not* reference selling. It's taking the time to match up your prospect with a current client where there is a major connection. What you're aiming for is a personality match as well as an industry match. Sometimes it's difficult to get both. This may mean you need to go outside your sales territory to find a match.

Once you determine the reference you want to use, it's time to focus on the venue. I've done field trips to the reference site, dinners, lunches, ball games, and golf outings. Do whatever works for both parties. Obviously the more quality time you have together the better.

One thing you must keep in mind is you must allow your prospect and reference some private time together to talk. This means you need to excuse yourself at some point to allow this to happen. For obvious reasons there needs to be interaction without the presence of a salesperson.

Years ago, when I attended DPMA (Data Processing Management Association) meetings on Thursday evenings, I would always try to connect a happy client with a prospect. I would go to buy drinks at the bar and position myself in such a way that I could introduce my prospect to my customer. Then I would ask my client to tell the prospect about our product and company in a casual and nonthreatening way. I would almost joke about it. Then I would say, "I'm going to leave you guys alone to chat because I don't want to influence the conversation." You know what they say: all salesmen are full of s…

Remember the old saying: "There is no better salesman than a satisfied customer." Never forget that! Use your satisfied customers as sale folks. But don't abuse this tool. And take care of them in some way for assisting you. If done effectively, 90 percent of the real selling will be done by your reference. It's a beautiful thing. In addition it's a lot of fun and accelerates the sales process.

Market share-As a professional sales rep, you should know certain facts relative to where your company fits in the overall market. If you work for a small supplier in a regional market, you should have a good idea as to what market share you have in that area. If you work for a large manufacturer, you should know your market share nationwide as well as where you stand locally.

Market share is an ever-moving target and can be confusing. For example in the mid '90s EMC was taking market share away from IBM in a big way. So I referred to *new shipments* in terms of our market share. The reason is if you take into consideration installed systems as well as new shipments, it would take years for EMC to surpass IBM, who'd had twenty-plus years to ship and install storage systems. The fact that EMC shipped and delivered more than IBM in 1998, for example, was a very compelling statistic. The currently installed storage was a static number we had no influence over. The fact that most new orders for data storage were going to EMC was a powerful statement. We had no market share in terms of new shipments in 1991, and in 1998 we shipped more storage to IBM mainframe accounts than IBM did. This was truly an amazing statistic, and something we needed to share on every possible occasion.

Service and support-Clients want to know what to expect after the sale is made. The service and support component varies significantly from industry to industry. For example if you work for a paper supplier, it only matters that you get the product delivered on time and your customer service department is available to handle any issues relative to the accuracy and or damage of the shipment. Outside of that there is very little ongoing service and support to evaluate.

Conversely, with the data storage systems I sold, ongoing service and support was a major consideration and in fact separated EMC from the competition. It was a component of the sale that we emphasized. We had call-home capabilities that automatically dialed our support center in Hopkinton, Massachusetts, in the event of a component failure. This was unique to EMC at the time. So you bet we talked about it.

Some products are differentiated from the competition completely by the company's service and support capabilities. If you're selling a generic product then possibility this is the only area where you can separate yourself. An example might be you want to purchase a new Chrysler 300. You make your choice of dealers because of one's service reputation. You might even decide to drive a bit farther in order to receive a higher level of service and support.

In the IT industry, we have a term called *VAR*. It stands for value added reseller. Manufactures typically sell their products to various VARs in a particular territory. Very rarely are there specific territories where VARs have exclusive rights. The VARs might represent various hardware and software products that are identical to those that are available from other VARS in the same territory. So the *only* differentiations between one VAR and the other are price, service, and support. The quality of the technical folks on staff at a successful VAR is a key component of success.

Your experience-Don't minimize your experience as an added-value component of the total package you represent. As a professional sales executive, you bring an abundance of knowledge and experience to the table. Your insight in terms of industry trends, competition, and overall consulting has *value*. In some cases you can offer information the client would need to pay for if you did not provide it.

For example in my role selling IBM-compatible displays, tape drives, and storage systems, I naturally learned a lot about the way IBM did business. One of my strengths was that I was the constant on the account for many years. IBM would frequently change sales reps. This meant the client needed to spend time educating the new IBM rep regarding the way they liked to do business. This took time, and in many cases the client was hesitant to put forth a lot of effort because the rep may have been replaced in twelve to eighteen months.

Continuity is an important ingredient for major clients. From my standpoint I was fortunate that IBM didn't recognize the importance of this. The IBM sales and support model became easy to figure out. I would therefore educate my clients in terms of how IBM would respond to a competitive threat from my company. It was quite predicable. And when I educated my clients in terms of how they could get more value from IBM by deploying my products, it resonated with them. I became more of a trusted advisor than a sales rep!

This happens over time when you are the constant on the account and your competitor continues to change reps. When a client recognizes the additional industry and consulting value you offer, they will go out of their way to give you every opportunity to win their business.

Your product relative to the competition-In most circles this is called your *competitive advantage* or your *unique selling promise*. It goes without saying that you'd better be very crisp with this message. For example if someone asks you what you do for a living, you should be able to articulate the answer in a few sentences that are easy to understand. This is called the *elevator pitch*, meaning in the time it takes an elevator to reach the destination floor you should have delivered your message.

The message should address a problem your product solves as well as your competitive advantage. The purpose is to create interest in learning more. It is not intended to sell the product on the spot. As an example if I ran into an executive at a major account while I represented Telex Computer Products and he asked me who I was and what Telex did, I might have said, "I'm Scott Dunkel with Telex. My company manufactures and services displays and printers that attach to your IBM mainframe computer. The devices are one hundred percent compatible and offer significant advantages in terms of price, delivery in addition to some unique capabilities." This is a high-level message intended to pique interest. When our first meeting was scheduled I would get into the particulars of Telex's competitive advantages. Back then we had many:

> *Price*: our products were less expensive than IBM's.

> *Delivery*: we could ship and install several weeks faster than IBM could.

> *Functionality*: we had certain capabilities that were unique to Telex.

As a professional sales executive, it is your responsibility to understand what your major competitive advantage is relative to your prospect's issues and problems. Price and delivery may not be important, but a unique feature or function may seal the deal.

In the late '70s Telex had a daisy wheel printer that attached directly to the IBM mainframe computer. IBM only had a dot matrix printer. It was faster than the Telex daisy wheel printer, but the daisy wheel had typewriter-like quality. If you remember, back in the late '70s people used typewriters for much of the correspondence we do via e-mail today. Executive assistants would actually type individual letters, make copies for the files, and send the originals off in the mail. I know this is hard to believe for folks who are under thirty.

IBM, by the way, was the largest supplier of typewriters back then. It was a huge part of their business. IBM then developed word-processing software that ran on their mainframe.

This meant executive assistants could use the display terminals IBM *and* TELEX offered to write letters. Remember, most everyone was using typewriters, not displays, to write letters.

But here was the problem: if the idea was to give folks the impression that the letter was coming out of a typewriter and not a computer, the dot matrix printer was a dead giveaway. And Telex was the only vendor that offered a high-quality printer that attached to an IBM mainframe. So it was our responsibility as professional sales reps to find out what IBM mainframe accounts in our territory had this word processing software installed. One account I identified was Michelin Tire. Their data center was on Long Island. When I met with the folks there, they were very excited to learn about our daisy wheel printer. My challenge was I didn't have any installed in the word processing environment in which they planned to deploy it. So I made some phone calls to find out where Telex had this printer installed in the same software environment as Michelin Tire. I found that Conrail in Philadelphia was a perfect match. David, the sales rep there, suggested we take the folks from Michelin on a field trip to visit the site and speak firsthand with the technical folks. So we got on an Amtrak and went down to Philly to spend the day with Conrail. (This is also an example of reference selling, mentioned above.)

The trip went well. When a happy customer does the selling, it's a beautiful thing. It wasn't long before we received an order for several printers. Additionally, since we offered display units as well, Michelin began to order those along with the printers. The point is we got into Michelin because of our unique competitive advantage with the daisy wheel printer. However, once in the door, we did significant business across various product lines moving forward.

In summary, it is critical to understand how your competitive advantage will benefit your prospect by solving a problem .In order to do this you must understand your competition's features, functions, benefits, and so on. If you don't, how can you position your product effectively? Take the necessary time to learn your competition. Then figure out how your product or service can provide advantages to your prospect that your competitor can't. If you do the research and honestly determine that your product or service has no compelling advantage, you will be fighting an uphill battle. You might consider a move to the competition.

CHAPTER REVIEW

- Be a student of your product or service.
- Understand your competition.
- Be able to articulate your competitive advantage.
- Understand and be able to represent your company from a corporate perspective.
- Be aware of industry trends.

CHAPTER 3

KNOW WHO YOU'RE CALLING ON

If you walked into a car dealership and went up to a salesman and asked him some questions about a car you had an interest in, and the *first* thing he said to you was, "Let's sit down and get to know one another before I tell you about my vehicles," what would your response be? You would most likely think something was wrong with this guy. You just wanted to get a few questions answered and maybe take a test drive.

Let's take this scenario one step further for fun. How about if you sat down with him and he knew the following information about you? Remember, this was the first time you met him.

Your name
Your wife's name
Your children's names
Your hobbies
Your income
Your monthly budget
Your previous car acquisitions
If you typically lease, purchase, or finance
What you owe on your current vehicle

How long you typically keep a car
The specific use of the car you're interested in purchasing
The creature features that excite you
Your driving habits
If you do a lot of winter driving
The typical number of people you chauffeur
How important gas mileage is to you
If you value high performance over safety
How you value service

Do you think a salesman armed with this data would have a better chance of making a sale than one who knows absolutely nothing about the prospect who just walked in? Obviously the chances of a car salesman knowing this much detail about a prospect is slim to none. I use this as a gross example to make my point.

But what if the salesman knew details about the prospect's family and referred to them by name? What if he understood what vehicles the prospect had purchased in the past and which he preferred? Or the type of driving he did and whether or not he liked high performance or fuel mileage? The salesman would have a much better chance at suggesting the vehicle that made the most sense. Additionally, don't you think the prospect would value the fact that the salesman took the time to understand the specifics of how he would utilize his new car? What his likes and dislikes were? Not to mention the fact that he knew the names of his family members. In fact I would venture to say the prospect would almost feel an obligation to do business with a salesman who went out of his way to understand his needs fully.

Now let's take this concept and apply it to corporate sales. The principle is the same: information and knowledge about your prospect will allow you to craft a proposal that specifically addresses the wants and needs of your client.

The title of this chapter is "Know Who You're Calling On." Your prospect is the person you're calling on, and so is the company he works for. I say this because it's equally important to understand the corporate culture and business drivers of the company as well as the individual personalities of the folks you're calling on. For example if you take the time to understand the individual and his or her needs and wants fully but fail to understand the business drivers of the company, your proposal might not get approved.

Perhaps a few real-life examples from my sales career will help clarify these principles. Back in 1979 I began a sales campaign with Citibank Credit Card Services (CCCS). They were the division of Citibank that issued Visa and MasterCard credit cards. Back in the late 1970s the credit card business was growing by leaps and bounds. CCCS, based in Long island, New York, was positioned to take advantage of this growth industry and add significant profitability to its parent company.

I was fortunate to have CCCS on my prospect list, and began a sales campaign. I represented Telex computer products at the time. Telex manufactured a 3270 display terminal. It was functionally equivalent to an IBM 3270 display terminal. Basically it provided the same functionality as the IBM product.

There was one major exception: Telex could deliver the product in thirty to sixty days. IBM at the time had a major backlog and was quoting lead times of close to a year. The demand for online terminals in the late 1970s could not keep up with supply. Telex was in an excellent position to capitalize on this IBM weakness in terms of lead times. There were several other competitors that manufactured 3270-compatible displays that worked well and could be delivered in less time than IBM as well.

As Citibank's credit card division continued to grow, so did its need for 3270 display terminals. These devices were critical for the customer service folks to authorize transactions. At that time many authorizations happened directly, with an individual on the telephone while looking at a 3270 display screen. While fast delivery provided Telex with a significant competitive advantage, there were many IBM mainframe customers that would not buy any device not manufactured by IBM. That company's salesmen would make all kinds of statements about possible compatibility issues and service problems in order to get clients to wait for their deliveries. IBM would also shuffle some deliveries in order to keep major accounts happy.

Since Citibank Credit Card Services was a major account, IBM was laser-focused on keeping competitors out for fear that significant 3270 business would be lost if one of us got a foothold. I began calling on Bob, an assistant vice president in charge of evaluating most of the hardware acquisitions at CCCS. We installed a demo unit for testing. As I recall there were two other competitors being evaluated at the same time.

Bob reported to Bill, CCCS's vice president, and Bill reported to Jenine, the senior vice president. Bob and I got along well. He liked my product and would recommend up the line that it performed well. I attempted to set up a meeting with Bob's boss, but was not successful. However, I had several casual conversations in the hall with Bill and attempted to find out how we were doing in the evaluation process and what if anything I could do to help them make a decision in Telex's favor.

Bill had kind of a cold personality. He wasn't a bad person, but I knew he would be difficult to make a connection with. One day while talking to Bob in order to get some help with Bill, he mentioned that Jenine pretty much made all the big decisions there anyway, so I might as well just wait and see how this exhaustive evaluation went and then try to meet directly with her. The evaluation would most likely take several months. I was not interested in sitting on my hands for that long and then potentially learning that we'd lost the business.

I asked Bob what was Jenine like. He told me she was a very smart, polished ,and well-respected senior executive. She was on a fast track at the bank and was well thought of throughout the organization. He also mentioned that she loved to play tennis. A couple of days later, I ran into her in the hall. I introduced myself and told her I was involved in an evaluation of 3270 terminals and would be happy to answer any questions she might have regarding Telex or its product. She was polite but appeared not interested in continuing to talk much more. Then I mentioned that Bob had told me she liked to play tennis.

She said, "I sure do," and her face lit up.

I responded with, "We should play sometime." Now, I still can't believe I was asking this senior vice president who I'd just casually met to play tennis. I would say Jenine was in her early forties, and I was twenty-five. Right after the words came out of my mouth, I felt embarrassed that I'd asked. But it was too late to take it back.

Guess what? To my surprise her response was, "Do you want to get beat?"

I said, "Sure. I have no problem getting beat." But I still wasn't sure if she was serious.

Turned out she *was* very serious—she had me arrange a time through her secretary that would be convenient. She was a member of a local indoor tennis club about five minutes from her office.

About a week later we got together to play our first match. Jenine was a skilled tennis player, and as you can imagine extremely competitive. We played for about an hour before she needed to get back to work, and as I recall she won our first match. Going forward we played tennis about once a week. I won some and she won some. Every match was close, but more importantly we enjoyed the competition as well as each other's company.

Jenine knew that my wife- to- be , Jackie, had gotten me involved in tennis and in fact worked for the USTA in New York at the time. Jackie arranged to secure four tickets to the US Open that year, and the four of us —Jackie, me, Jenine, and her husband Bob—spent a night watching *real* tennis players compete at Flushing Meadows. Then we went out to dinner and back to their house. After that we all got together to play mixed doubles a few times. I enjoyed talking with Bob, who had his own printing and binding business in Long Island. He invited me to his place of business for a tour. I had always had an interest in business and had lots of questions, which he patiently answered.

Remember, Jenine and Bob were in their forties at the time. Jackie and I were in our mid-twenties, so they could have been our parents. We all got along very well and enjoyed each other's company. Now, understand I was also very excited that Jackie and I had established this personal relationship with the senior vice president of Citicorp. And she was the one ultimately deciding on whether or not Telex would do business at the account. Talk about mixing business with pleasure! I had heard the term before, but this was my first real experience.

Quite frankly I was a bit nervous about how this relationship would transfer into business. I continued to call on Bob, who was running the evaluation as well as some of the other folks below him who were more of the technical type. I never made it a point to mention that I had established a personal relationship with Jenine. I suppose I was concerned I would be viewed differently by her underlings.

One day I was talking with Jenine in her office about our evaluation. I was by no means giving her a sales pitch. She called Bill into her office. Remember, Bill was Bob's boss and basically made all hardware recommendations to Jenine. When Bill walked in, she asked if he knew me. Bill mentioned very casually that he did. However, that was about it. He and I had not established any business relationship. He had been a bit unapproachable, so he really didn't know me at all.

Then Jenine said something like this to Bill: "Scott Dunkel is a friend of mine. He is the Telex rep. I like Scott very much, and I want you to do business with him!" I felt extremely uncomfortable as Jenine uttered those words, but Bill certainly got the message. It wasn't very long after that brief meeting that the orders started to roll in for our displays. Citicorp quickly became my largest account by far. In defense of Jenine, we did in fact have a very reliable and user-friendly product that we could deliver in a timely fashion. We also priced it competitively. Jenine did not get to her executive level position by making bad decisions. I'm sure she did her due diligence before instructing Bill to open up the floodgates.

However, I'm also convinced that she trusted me to make it right if there were issues with our product or service. The fact of the matter is my relationship with Jenine resulted in significant business for Telex. Additionally, having a household name as a reference significantly increases your chances of doing business with other large accounts — particularly in the banking industry.

The point of this story is to get you to THINK about accounts you are currently calling on or accounts you would like to call on that have high potential. Accounts you might feel a bit intimidated to call on for whatever reason. Accounts that seem to be off limits to you. Accounts other sales folks have told you "never by anything but XYZ product." Accounts where it's difficult to get meetings with the key decision makers. Accounts that might take a long time to penetrate and you feel you don't have the time to dedicate to them.

I hope you get my point. Don't assume any account in your territory is too big or too difficult to do business with. Remember, we all put our pants on the same way every morning. Individuals are individuals. The key to success is to learn what makes your prospect tick. What motivates her? What are her personal interests? What have other companies done to win her business? What type of sales approach does she feel comfortable with? What sports does she like? Does she hunt or fish?

Get the point? It's your responsibility as a professional to learn as much as you can about the decision maker. You learn that from the people who work for her. One of the best ways to gain information as well as meetings with the executive is to establish a strong relationship with her assistant. You would be surprised how much trust an executive puts in her assistant. Many times the assistant controls the executive's schedule.

Now, you might say, "I have such a superior product it will sell itself. All I need to do is get a meeting with the right person and I will be home free." In some cases that might be true. I would rather increase my chances of doing business by taking the time to learn about my prospect. This is particularly true when you represent a product or service that is more of a commodity. When you don't have a major competitive advantage, it behooves you to KNOW YOUR PROSPECT even more. After all, if you don't have a distinguishable competitive advantage then your relationship needs to be your competitive advantage. And how do you gain a relationship? By understanding your prospect in detail.

In my example with Citicorp, I found out the final decision maker loved tennis. That common ground allowed us to connect on a personal level. It is critical to make a connection with your prospect. That is the beginning of establishing your relationship. It could be a shared interest in sports, travel, skiing, family, etc. You and your prospect should enjoy your meetings together. If it is *all* business it is not a lot of fun for either of you. For example if you both like to ski, meet at the mountain one day and spend some time on the slopes together. Use this time to get to know your prospect and *not* to sell him. There is nothing worse than making a sales call when you and your prospect are out for a day of leisure. If your prospect asks you a business question, by all means answer it. But don't be the one to initiate the business discussion. Your mission is to connect in a non-business way.

Connection leads to **like**, which is one of the three reasons people do business. The other two are **trust** and **respect**. But before you can get to trust and respect, there needs to be a connection. And before there can be a connection, it is up to you to do the necessary research to KNOW YOUR PROSPECT!

Knowing your prospect functions on many different levels. As discussed above there is knowledge about his likes and dislikes, and then there are cultural differences depending on the part of the country in which he lives. As an example , when I called on accounts in New York City in the late '70s, I was a very green sales rep and did not do any research on my prospects before I made calls. I would march in and begin talking about my product with hopes of installing demo devices. In that way I learned that folks in NYC have little time to waste. If I did not get them interested in my product in the first five minutes, they pretty much showed me the door.

Thereafter, I had a very specific and direct pitch I executed that was all business. New York is a fast-paced business environment, and if you do not get your prospect's attention *very* quickly your chances of doing business are small. Conversely, when I relocated to Maryland and began dealing with prospects the way I had done in New York, it did not go over very well. My customers and prospects asked me to slow down and take a breath. Suffice it to say the New York attitude did not go over very well. Thankfully it only took me a few months to realize I needed to change my approach significantly if I expected to be successful in Maryland.

It is true that people operate differently depending on location. The fact of the matter is *you* need to be able to read your prospect in terms of how you can make the best connection. I always prefer to find some common ground independent of business that we can both relate to. Items in his office might give you clues, such as pictures of the executive skiing or golfing, or some sort of sports memorabilia for example. As I did with Jenine, you can also ask other folks in the organization about your prospect's areas of interest.

Back in the late '90s, when I was a leasing manager for Memorex/Telex, I flew down to Nashville to work with a rep on a tape-drive deal. The story sticks in my mind because it was an extreme case of how some folks prefer to discuss business. We had a lunch meeting with the account on a Tuesday, to be followed the next day by a meeting at the office. We spent about an hour talking at lunch about the prospect's family as well as other non-business topics. The customer excused himself to use the restroom, and I asked Bob, the sales rep, when we were going to talk about the deal. Bob said we were not going to talk *any* business at lunch. His customer did not like to talk business while out of the office. The lunch was only meant to introduce me and get him comfortable with me, so we could have a more productive meeting the next day.

It would be rare for something like this to happen in the Northeast region of the country, where the pace is much faster, and lunches and dinners are typically used to accomplish business objectives. Again, it's up to you to determine the most effective approach and execute it.

Another example of knowing your customer was related to me by a senior sales exec I used to work with.

In 1999 Diane, a sales exec with EMC, sold several large Symmetrix storage systems to PSI Net. As you may recall, this was the dotcom era. Internet service providers (ISPs) were the wave of the future. It looked like there was no end in sight in terms of growth.

The customer, PSI Net, was delighted with the performance, reliability, and space-saving attributes of the EMC storage product. They wanted to position their company for future growth as they expanded worldwide. To this end they contacted Diane to set up a high-level meeting. They asked her to bring in her manager as well as Dick, the CEO of EMC. The meeting took place in a large conference room at PSI Net's headquarters in Northern Virginia. The president and owner as well as the company's IT executives were in attendance. After the initial introductions and pleasantries were exchanged, the president announced that he wanted to sign a volume purchase agreement (VPA) with EMC. If you are a sales exec, a sales manager, or the CEO of EMC, this is certainly music to your ears. Immediately after he made this announcement, Dick pounded his fist on the table and said, "How about thirty million dollars?"

The room was silent for what felt like an eternity. Then the president of PSI Net said, "How about one hundred million?"

Needless to say the EMC team was shocked. Thirty million seemed like a huge commitment for PSI Net to make. After the meeting, when the EMC team thought through the forecasted growth, the $100 million commitment, did, in fact make sense. The plan was to replicate more than thirteen data centers worldwide. So logically the $100 million VPA was accurate. Unfortunately, it turned out that PSI Net was one of the dotcom casualties—they filed for bankruptcy and are no longer in business. They did, however, purchase and pay for the original $30 million deal.

So the lesson learned here is quite basic, but nevertheless critical: before you begin any negotiation, do the necessary research to understand the needs of your client. Don't make assumptions—especially if they are too low! Knowing your customer means doing the necessary research in advance of a high-level meeting. This is especially true if you're inviting senior executives to join you. An example would be if you do the math and determine that the customer would need eighty million in product over a thirty-six month period. Then I would ask for a VPA of one hundred million, the idea being it is much better to shoot high and have the client bring you back down to earth.

In addition to connecting and building trusting business relationships with the various individuals within an organization, it is important to understand the *culture* of the company you're calling on. Just as people have likes and dislikes and prefer to be approached in different ways, so do the companies they work for! Companies have personalities, often referred to as the *corporate culture*, and it can be extremely helpful to understand them. If you present a proposal that your primary contact supports but it doesn't match up with the culture of the organization, it will most assuredly be rejected.

You can learn a lot about a company's corporate culture by reading its annual report or by going to its website. Additionally, you can talk with folks within the organization to get a sense of what the corporation values. For example, what is its mission statement? What does the CEO talk about in terms of corporate values? What are the future plans of the company? How do they intend to grow revenue? What is their core competency? Do they place a high value on employee loyalty? Are they willing to invest to gain a clear competitive advantage, or do they want to be the low-cost provider? How much do they spend on advertising?

You get the point. By understanding the corporate culture from the top down, you will be much better positioned to present a proposal that will be well received.

As an example I called on two accounts for many years whose corporate cultures were as different as night and day. I'm not suggesting one was right and the other was wrong. I'm suggesting it is beneficial to understand the landscape in which you're working. The two accounts were GEICO and T. Rowe Price. Both were very successful. Both have grown in market share over the last ten years, GEICO in the insurance industry and T. Rowe Price in the mutual fund and 401(k) servicing industry.

When you walk through the doors of GEICO's corporate headquarters outside of Washington, DC, you feel as if you're going back in time. The lobby and reception area feels very cold. The couches are black vinyl, and the floors are industrial-looking. It almost feels like the lobby of some sort of manufacturing plant or high school. It is hard to describe. It simply is not very inviting.

The executive offices are similar: poor lighting along with furniture that is outdated and not very ergonomic. When you enter a conference room, the tables and chairs are cobbled together. In other words it is apparent that a complete conference room table and chair combination was not a priority. One GEICO employee mentioned to me that it's hard to find two matching chairs in any conference room! When walking through the halls, you get the distinct feeling that you're in a 1970s-style building. This is especially true in the restrooms. They are extremely dark and, in my opinion, a bit depressing. The employees talk about the need to work long hours in order to get their work done.

The company does, however, seem to retain its employees. In fact several of the folks I called on had been with GEICO for more than twenty-five years. So apparently they didn't see value in updating their office environment. They saw value in spending millions of dollars a year on advertising. I would venture to say that you can't watch an hour of television without seeing a GEICO commercial. Or seeing a billboard for GEICO while driving down the road. They certainly value advertising, and it must be working or they would not continue to do it.

T. Rowe Price, on the other hand has invested significantly in providing a bright and cheery office environment. From the minute you enter the lobby, it is obvious they are interested in projecting a certain high-quality and successful image. A high degree of attention was paid to every detail in the reception area. The conference rooms have matching furniture and offer state-of-the art audio/visual technology. It is a very comfortable environment in which to work. When talking to employees, you don't get the impression that they are being worked to death. High-quality work is expected but should be accomplished during normal business hours.

T. Rowe Price, like GEICO, has many long-term employees. T. Rowe spends money on advertising but has a completely different message. Think about the two tag lines that are typically used by these companies:

GEICO: "15 minutes can save you 15 percent or more on car insurance."

T. Rowe Price: "Invest with confidence"

One is based on price and the other is based on quality. Does this not speak volumes about their corporate cultures? T. Rowe is not going after the high-volume stock trader who is looking to make several trades a day and is looking for the lowest-cost provider. They are interested in establishing long-term relationships with their clients that are based on trust. GEICO is interested in luring you away from your current insurance provider by offering a lower price.

And guess what? As a vendor who's sold to both of these companies, I can tell you firsthand that this corporate culture trickles down to the decision makers. When dealing with GEICO, if you can show them a way to save money you have a good chance of getting their attention. When dealing with T. Rowe Price, if you can show them a way to improve their service to their clients you have a good chance of winning their business. I'm not saying price is not important to T. Rowe and quality is not important to GEICO. What I am saying is understanding the culture in terms of what to lead with is critical.

In my experience with both accounts, it became obvious that T. Rowe valued its trusted relationships with its vendors more than GEICO did. With GEICO, if you did not continue to be the low-cost provider, there was a good chance you would lose the business. T. Rowe looked to its vendors to provide more than the lowest price. Again, I'm not saying one is right and one is wrong. Both companies are successful, and understanding the corporate culture from a high level will give you the best chance for success. Take the time to understand it and use it to your advantage.

CHAPTER REVIEW

- Determine how to make an initial connection with your prospect.
- Understand the culture of your account.
- Work on building trust and respect.
- Understand your prospect's business drivers.

CHAPTER 4

THE ART OF LISTENING

In all seriousness, there is no single aspect of professional selling more important than developing effective listening habits. This is true not only in sales but in life in general. God gave us two ears and one mouth for good reason. Yet for some strange reason many sales folks feel the need to talk more than listen. I suppose it goes with the territory of being a salesperson. We sometimes feel people expect us to be outgoing and always chewing someone's ear off.

If you have read traditional sales technique books, they talk about continuing to talk past the point of sale. This is when your prospect tells you he would like to purchase your product, but instead of proceeding with the required paperwork to finalize the transaction you can't help but continue to explain other features of the product. He then hears something come out of your mouth that discourages him from continuing with the purchase. Maybe a feature you think is great is something he dislikes, so he changes his mind. This is a gross example of not listening. After all, if your objective is to sell, and the prospect tells you he wants to buy, then why are you still talking?

As a professional salesperson your objective is to solve your clients' problems with your product or service. This should not be a news flash. Any book on selling will tell you that. Yet how can you solve your prospects' problems if you don't know what they are? Too many times you sit down with your prospect and begin by telling him how great your company and products are. You go through a canned presentation that might take an hour to present and feel delighted that you manage to get through the entire thing without one single question. When asked how the meeting went, you tell your manager it went great, and you are fairly sure you will be doing business with the prospect in the future. You've convinced yourself that if your prospect listened to your entire pitch, he's convinced you have a great product and will soon be ordering. Your presentation is so compelling, the prospect may have faxed in an order by now.

What you don't realize is your prospect most likely doesn't remember much if anything from your presentation. In fact if he didn't ask any questions, that's a sure sign your presentation did not address any compelling needs he might have had. Statistics indicate that even if your prospect was intrigued by your presentation, he would still forget much of it after you left the office. Yet many sales folks are compelled to get through their PowerPoint's by hook or by crook. We have *our* agenda. We are convinced we know what's right for the prospect, and if they listen to our presentations they will get it and buy our product or service.

Kevin, the former CIO at Allegis Group, related a story wherein a salesperson was moving through his presentation in a rapid fashion due to a time constraint. Kevin politely interrupted him and said he was not interested in the particular software the salesperson was presenting but *was* interested in another software product that the vendor offered. Kevin expected the sales rep to move on to the other product, but instead he finished the presentation on the product in which Kevin had no interest. This scenario is unfortunately repeated over and over by sales folks. On almost every interview I've had with key decision makers, I've heard the same story. Is it that we don't listen, or are we so convinced that if we get through our prepared presentations, our prospects will finally see the light? Why wouldn't we take the time to listen to what the prospect would like to purchase? Why do we sometimes think *we* know what the prospect wants to purchase?

Kevin related another story wherein he invited his strategic partners in for a meeting to review the plans for the upcoming year, including the products and services they will purchase that year. Would you believe some vendors do not show up for this discussion? Your customer is taking the time to share his plan with you so you will know where to focus your energy in order to meet his needs. He is essentially laying out for you on a silver platter his strategic plan and how he and his team have decided to spend their budget. He values you enough to include you in this meeting. And you decide it's not important? This is a true story, and I can only assume it happens all the time.

So let's get back to the whole point of this chapter. If you are to solve a prospect's problem with your product or service, you first need to understand what the problem is. Logically this means you can't march into his office and make a presentation. Why? Because you don't know what to present. Not all prospects have the same problems. They may be similar, but you will never know for sure unless you know how to ask the right questions and then sit back and listen. So before you march in with your perfect presentation, the first step should be to understand what challenges and issues this prospect is facing. Depending on the account and organization structure, this might involve several meetings to understand fully the business issues.

In my career I would ask probing questions regarding IT challenges my prospect might have been facing. Some examples:

- Is the company having application performance issues?
- Are their backup windows too tight?
- Are they running into business continuance challenges?
- Are there space constraints in their computer room?

WHAT THEY DON'T TEACH YOU IN SALES SCHOOL

Based on the answers to these questions as well as discussions with my technical team (since I was never very technical), I would come up with some more detailed questions I would ask at our next meeting. I would not come in with a canned presentation; instead I would begin the process of specifically identifying the issue I believed our product would address. Again this would involve very specific questions that would help our account team get a firm grasp on the business challenge. We would all continue to do a lot more listening then speaking.

As they say, knowledge is power. The more you know, the more you can effectively articulate your prospect's issues back to him along with the potential solution you're offering. In other words you can explain in detail that you fully understand what the problem is, then ask for acknowledgement that you are correct in your assessment. Then you can present your proposal to solve the problem. When your prospect knows you took the necessary time to *listen*, he will naturally feel you sincerely care about him and are not simply trying to fit your solution to his problem.

Bob, a former VP at Citigroup, related a story of a software salesman. It seemed whatever technical challenge Bob was facing, this particular sales rep had the best solution! Bob would describe an issue he was attempting to solve. The salesman would say, "We have the software to fix that." Bob would describe another problem totally unrelated to the first. The salesman would say, "We have another product to solve that." The rep essentially had a solution to *every* problem Bob had. And all without learning the technical details of the problem! Needless to say a sales rep that operates like this does not inspire confidence.

Let's dig a bit deeper and use a real-life example to illustrate how to combine the correct questions with effective listening skills. The more knowledge you uncover by utilizing effective listening and follow-up questions, the better prepared you will be to formulate a compelling proposal. Some salespeople stop their interactions prior to understanding the entire business challenge. They rush to the proposal stage and, many times, ask for the order before enough valuable data is uncovered.

As an EMC sales exec, I sold data storage that was capable of supporting IBM mainframe applications, all flavors of UNIX, and Microsoft Windows. In addition EMC offered a whole host of software products to enhance these storage systems. In 1993, when I started with the company, we only offered data storage that supported IBM mainframe applications. It essentially emulated IBM 3390 storage and attached directly to the IBM mainframe.

The easiest way to sell our product was to bring it in on evaluation. So, in the fall of 1993, we arranged to bring our system, called Symmetrix, into Blue Cross Blue Shield of the National Capital Area. The company is currently called CareFirst Blue Cross Blue Shield. In any event, the first night they ran their batch processing workload, it completed several hours ahead of schedule. My prospect called me, sounding very concerned. He thought something was wrong. He thought there was no way the job could have completed that quickly. We dispatched our technicians to the account to review the logs. They determined everything was fine—the EMC storage was simply that much faster. Needless to say Blue Cross was very impressed.

Now, decisions at large accounts don't happen overnight. In fact when it comes to replacing IBM data storage with another vendor, it can become quite political. We were fortunate to move the purchasing process along at a fairly good pace. As I recall we received our first order late in 1993 for the 180 gigabyte Symmetrix. The 180GB sounds puny now, but believe me when I tell you that was a lot of data storage back then. The price was more than a million dollars as well.

Based on several meetings and discussions, we were actively positioning EMC for all the new growth at Blue Cross. The first order of 180GB was certainly significant. However, our objective was to be the preferred supplier of data storage for all *new* storage requirements. To this end we met with the folks who had visibility to future application requirements as well as general data base growth, etc. These were different folks from those we had originally worked with for the evaluation and original contract negotiation. So our questions and listening skills were honed in on all the important information that would allow us to formulate a compelling proposal for *all* of their combined growth over the next year. This information would allow us to offer more aggressive pricing that took into consideration a much larger financial commitment.

During this period the first Symmetrix was performing perfectly. It was physically much smaller than the IBM 3390 system. It used less power, and obviously was significantly faster. The Blue Cross executives would be recommending the use of EMC for all future purchases.

Our sales team listened effectively and positioned EMC for a great future at Blue Cross. But instead of being satisfied with future storage requirements; what if we could replace existing IBM 3390 storage? I began to work with some of the folks who had information regarding the currently installed storage. We found out that Blue Cross owned all of the 3390 storage that was currently installed in their data center. I asked the key decision maker if he would be interested in replacing a large portion of it with EMC storage if I could do it at no cost. He said, "Of course," but looked at me like I was crazy. I knew what he was thinking: how could this possibly be done?

Now, I didn't know if I could pull this off, but it was certainly worth a try. But before I could begin working on the deal, I had to get confirmation from the customer that he **would** be willing to do the swap. I would then go back to my management and present the opportunity. From my experience in the computer-leasing business, I was very familiar with how the process worked. There were several brokers who bought used IBM storage. The question was whether or not they would pay enough to cover the cost of the new EMC product.

The good news for us back in 1993 was that the market for used 3390 data storage was still vibrant. EMC was new to the business, and there were plenty of IBM mainframe customers that would prefer to purchase used 3390s on the open market than pay retail for new ones. We orchestrated a deal where we took several strings of IBM 3390 disk drives out and replaced them with new EMC Symmetrix at absolutely no cost to Blue Cross. The customer couldn't have been happier. And EMC received an additional contract for just north of a million dollars. This all came about because we continued to ask questions in addition to thinking outside of the box. Many of these principles are outlined in the "Financial Sale" chapter.

Today's IT environment is much more complex, and vendors offer a wide variety of solutions to the same business challenge. In 1993 EMC offered IBM mainframe data storage with one performance level. That was it—period. Today an EMC rep must drill down very deep to gather as much knowledge as possible regarding the client's business challenges. Therefore his or her ability to ask questions and be an effective listener is more crucial than ever. If, for example, a sales exec is given a lead that client XYZ is in need of 500GB of capacity for their IBM mainframe, the probing questions he would ask are significantly different from what I asked back in 1993.

Regardless of the complexity of the product, you must still understand your audience. When discussing your product and company with senior executives, you should focus on *business* issues. When talking with more technical folks, your focus should be on the *technical* aspects of your product—as we used to call it the "speeds and feeds." Techies want to learn how fast the disk drive spins, the amount of cache memory, the data transfer rate, the redundant components, etc. On the other hand the executive wants to know your product is going to make his company more profitable by making or saving money. He obviously needs to get the OK from the techies that it will work and be reliable, but he typically is not interested in the technical details. So don't spend a lot of time in that area with him.

During your meeting with an executive-level person who is interested in 500GB of storage for his mainframe, you would want to ask questions like this and listen carefully to his responses:

- What application will this new data storage support?
- Is this an existing or a new application?
- How mission-critical is this application?

- Will high-performance storage result in increased revenue? If so how would you measure it?
- What type of growth do you forecast?
- If this is mission-critical, how do you plan on backing it up?
- Explain your current DR and business continuance strategies.
- If the application goes down, do you know how much revenue loss you will incur per hour?
- Are there other applications on the mainframe that are growing as well? If so when would you foresee additional storage requirements coming into play?
- Do you have other computing platforms such as UNIX or Microsoft Windows?

(You would ask similar questions as you did for the mainframe applications above.)

In your meeting with the technical folks you would have a series of questions related to the technical aspects of their environment. The questions you ask will allow you to formulate your solution to address any technical concerns they may have.

The point here is that you are in information-gathering mode. Notice that you made no mention of your product or service! You are not in a position of selling until you learn the environment and fully understand the business challenges your prospect faces. I use the above questions as examples. Every business is certainly different, and every question might generate another question, so you might be drilling down very deep on several questions. That's OK. The more your prospect talks and you don't, the more you learn.

What I might do after gathering this data is ask your prospect what vendor he is currently using. You could ask what he likes and dislikes about his current provider, but be careful not to badmouth. Although it can be tempting, you should *never* speak unfavorably about your competitor. Allow your prospect to vent, but don't throw wood on the fire. This is unprofessional, and you never know—you might work for that competitor in the future. Simply understand as much as you can without making your prospect feel uncomfortable.

In summary, the more your prospect talks about his environment and business challenges, the better prepared you will be to formulate a winning proposal. Before your meeting, do your research and think of questions that require more than a yes or no response—questions that require your prospect to think and respond with information that will help you to understand fully the specific challenges he faces. The conversation should be natural, with each question leading to a follow-up question. It should not come off as a list of questions you have prepared in advance and you're simply going down it one at a time.

You might start the conversation out something like this: "Mr. Prospect, you are a very busy man. I don't want to waste your valuable time by presenting a proposal that doesn't meet your needs. If you would be kind enough to share with me the business challenges you're facing, I will do my best to formulate a solution."

Now, begin to listen carefully and have follow-up questions. Additionally, your demeanor and posture should be nonthreatening. This should be a natural conversation that puts your client at ease. It should not come off as an attorney doing a cross-examination. This is very important!

In most cases he will tell you what he needs. Don't jump to conclusions and start selling immediately! Be patient and continue to listen.

CHAPTER REVIEW

- Ask thoughtful questions that will assist you in uncovering business challenges.
- Listen carefully to the answers.
- Don't interrupt!
- Don't be totally focused on your agenda.
- Adjust your discussion based on your client's answers.
- Apply your solutions to the client's problems.

CHAPTER 5

STEP OUT OF YOUR COMFORT ZONE AND SELL AT ALL LEVELS

Have you ever found yourself in a situation where you are stuck at a certain level in an account? It might be at a mid-level management position or perhaps even with a very low level technical person. Regardless, you feel the need to move up to the next level of decision making. The problem is you have spent quite a bit of time with your current contact, and at this point you are uncomfortable with moving up the chain. Perhaps your current contact has indicated that his manager doesn't like dealing with sales reps, or maybe he flat-out told you not to go over his head. In any event you are frustrated with the progress (or lack thereof) you have made. You don't want to sacrifice your relationship with your current contact yet feel a need to deliver your message at a higher level.

This situation is very common and can be completely avoided in the future if you *start* at a high level. Depending on the size of the business you're calling on, this might mean calling on the owner or president. In my case I would begin calling on the chief information officer (CIO). There was certainly no reason for me to call on the president of T. Rowe Price or Citigroup, for example. So I would begin my campaign at the highest level within information technology. Since I was selling data storage, she would make the final decision regarding the products and services that were acquired. I knew the CIO would not be involved in the evaluation, and in most cases she would defer to middle management or even technical folks regarding these decisions.

The point is I wanted to establish some sort of working relationship with the *final* decision maker. There are several reasons for this.

1) The CIO would typically lay out her organization to me. In other words she would give me her organizational chart. This would help me navigate through the company. I would know all the important people I would need to establish relationships with. Many times the CIO would even lay out the decision-making process. This would save me a tremendous amount of time. I would know all the key folks to call on.

2) The CIO would typically tell me where to begin my selling campaign. It most likely would be with one of her direct reports who was responsible for data storage. Sometimes she would tell her direct report I would be calling him. Sometimes she simply told me to call him. In any case I would use the CIO as a reference to get my first meeting with this direct report.

3) During the selling process I can keep the entire management team in the loop regarding my progress *without* going over anyone's head. This is very important because in a very large account there might be three levels of management between the person evaluating my product and the CIO. If something is going askew, I have access to all levels of management without bruising anyone's ego.

4) The selling process is typically faster when you begin at the top. One way or the other, you will either do business

or not. Since time is your most valuable asset, you need to protect it. Spending time avoiding political situations and bruised egos is not productive.

We have certainly established that calling at a high-level accelerates the sales process and makes good use of your time. Now the question on your mind is: how do I do it? Maybe you're a young rep and feel uncomfortable calling on a senior executive. Fair enough. Let's spend some time dealing with this challenge.

The first thing you need to get over is the fact that senior-level executives are difficult to talk to. Conventional wisdom would tell you that you have nothing in common with them. If you're a junior sales rep, perhaps in your mid-twenties, and the individual ultimately responsible for purchasing your product or service is in his late fifties, you will be, by default, a bit nervous about the meeting. This executive may be three or four levels above the entry level person who is closer to your age and level of experience, so you naturally you'll convince yourself that you have no business calling on the executive.

Let me give you a news flash: the senior executive did not get to that level of management because he lacks people skills. My experience has been that the higher in the organization you call, the *easier* and more comfortable it is to have a conversation.

To drive this point home, I would like to relate a story from a round of golf that has had a profound impact on me for more than thirty years. One Saturday morning back in the mid–'80s, I got up early and decided to play a round of golf. My wife and I had recently joined a country club. The primary purpose for joining the club was that I needed to learn how to play golf. At least this is what several senior sales folks had told me. They'd said lots of business was done on the golf course, and I had better learn how to play the game.

Back then we had a very unusual way of setting up foursomes. There was a metal chute at the first tee. When you arrived you would place your ball in the chute. The golf pro would then set up foursomes based on the location of the balls in the chute. This meant there was a good chance you would get teamed up with different players every Saturday morning. Of course if four players all showed up together, then they would play together. But this method allowed for folks to meet other members and was in fact great for me, since I didn't know many members at the time.

On one particular Saturday morning, I was teamed with two other folks I had never met. One was Chris, and the other was George. We went out as a threesome. It was obvious that Chris and George knew each other. I was not sure if they were personal or business associates, but it was clear they had a solid relationship. They were both very pleasant to me. I was about thirty years their junior. In addition I was not a very good golfer, so they needed lots of patience. Incidentally, you still need to have patience with my golf game.

I'll never forget what happened as we were waiting to tee off on the thirteenth hole. George asked me what I did for a living. I told him I was a sales rep for Telex Computer Products and explained that we manufactured displays that attached to IBM mainframe computers. Being polite, I asked George what he did for a living. He told me he worked for Baltimore Gas & Electric (BGE). He just left it at that. No details, just that he worked for our local utility company.

As we were walking off the tee, Chris turned to me and said, "George is the president and CEO of BGE." He then told me he worked directly for George as a VP in charge of engineering and construction. So there I was, a twenty-eight-year-old salesman playing golf with the president and vice president of my local utility. They both were unpretentious. Easy to talk to. They didn't appear to have big egos and were humble. They had nothing to prove.

Coincidently I had been calling on BGE. They had a fairly large data center. In fact I had a demo unit installed at the time. I told George and Chris this, and they asked me who I was working with. I told them, and not surprisingly they had *no idea* who the guy was. He was about thirty-two levels below George.

What I should have done was ask George to broker a meeting with the CIO of BGE. But I was too young and inexperienced to think of it at the time. It certainly would have accelerated my opportunities at BGE. But that is not the point of this story. The point is: senior executives typically are easy folks to talk with. Most are personable and will listen to you if you have something of value to discuss.

These folks have less to prove than the lower-level guys, and since they're in charge of the whole operation they will be honest and less political regarding the organizational landscape. They will simply lay out the criteria regarding how they do business and point you in the direction where you should begin. Your meeting might be short, but if you come away with the organizational chart as well as the typical flow of business for your product set, it was a success.

So now we have established that senior executives are usually easy to talk with and will lay the foundation for your sales campaign. Now your challenge is to get the meeting. This, of course, is the difficult part, but by no means is it impossible. The first thing to keep in mind is that senior executives think in terms of *business issues*, not technical or product issues. When discussing your product or service with lower-level management or purchasing agents, the focus tends to be price, delivery, performance, features, etc. When meeting with senior executives you must shift your focus to business value. This is where the true professional distinguishes himself from the pack. In order to get a meeting with the senior executive you must determine how your product or service will impact his business. This may take some time and research, but it is absolutely necessary if you expect to have a successful first meeting.

Let me give you an example from my career. Hopefully this will resonate with you in terms of your product or service.

We were in the initial stages of a long sales campaign at T. Rowe Price in Baltimore, Maryland. The account had both IBM and HDS data storage installed at the time. Typically an account would either be all IBM or have a mix of IBM and one other plug-compatible manufacturer. Most large IBM shops would prefer not to have three storage vendors on the floor, so from my perspective if we were going to do business with T. Rowe on a large scale we would need to have a major competitive advantage—one so compelling they would be willing to make a move away from one of their current suppliers.

EMC had a distinct performance advantage over the two installed competitors. Additionally, we had some software capabilities that were totally unique and added value. While these features and benefits were selling points, they needed to be translated into real business value to T. Rowe. It's akin to offering a high-performance sports car to someone in downtown Manhattan—it may be really nice to have, but it provides little value over a Ford Fiesta based on the environment in which it will be driven.

So our task was to uncover an application where our data storage would make a significant impact. T. Rowe Price makes their money by managing money. The technical term is *assets under management*. They have a variety of mutual funds they offer their clients. The application and associated data were obviously mission-critical—so critical, in fact, they obviously needed to be backed up nightly. The challenge was that while it is being backed up, the application would not be available for access. In addition, since the application was growing, the nightly backup window was shrinking. In other words the time it took to back up the data base was getting very close to the opening of the stock market. The backup window was elongating to the point where it took almost all night, and there was no room for error. The online systems needed to be available first thing in the morning, and if the backup failed the company would not have an up-to-date copy of the data.

This was fast becoming a major concern for T. Rowe's management. Based on the speed of our storage, in addition to a unique software we offered, EMC had a solution. It was one thing to tell senior management at T. Rowe we believed we could solve the problem; it was quite another to convince them it would operate as advertised without any glitches for their most important application. Remember, we were talking about placing the company's most critical data on a non-SUN storage platform. They had a multitude of SUN servers and were exclusively using SUN data storage as well.

Decisions of this magnitude going wrong cause folks to lose their jobs. In order to get T. Rowe management comfortable, we modeled their environment at our lab in Hopkinton, Massachusetts. My systems engineer, along with a technical representative from T. Rowe, flew to Hopkinton and spent several days certifying the solution. It worked perfectly! Everyone was excited—especially yours truly, since this would be our first major order at this prestigious account.

When the system was installed in T. Rowe's environment, it worked like a charm. From that point forward, I believe, no further SUN storage was purchased. The lesson here is that many times the technical folks within an organization get comfortable with the current supplier. They understand how to manage and service the products and are not interested in learning new ones. So even if a vendor has a solution that is better, there may be some push back from the technical team.

This means it's necessary to sell the *business* value of the solution along with the technical capabilities. It was my responsibility to translate the performance aspects of the EMC data storage to real business value as it related to a mission-critical application. Business value resonates with folks in the IT organization who directly interface with the folks responsible for supporting business applications. And the business value can only be sold at a senior-management level. The ability to discuss how EMC technology could solve the backup window problem with VP-level management provided the opportunity for the EMC and T. Rowe technical teams to work together on the evaluation. Without buy-in from senior management, it never would have happened.

Let's take a look at another example from a completely different industry. A good friend of mine owns a manufacturing company in Maine. They have several very expensive C&C machines that can produce very precise components for various applications. Currently they do work in the aerospace industry and medical field.

Their equipment has a useful life, and therefore every five years or so they refresh one of the units. Typically an RFP goes out to several manufactures with a list of specifications that need to be met. Obviously the sales reps make personal calls on the individual soliciting the proposals. If the sales reps lock on the purchasing and technical folks within the company and don't elevate their proposals to the executive level, they are truly missing the boat. Here's why: If a manufacturer meets the specs of the RFP and is the lowest bidder, one would assume he would win the business. But what happens if a manufacturer *exceeds* the specs but is slightly higher than the lowest bidder? If they haven't been in front of senior management to explain the added value their product offers then they have no chance of winning the order.

This is particularly true if the new vendor would require training on their product. We all know folks don't like to change and learn new things, so if the incumbent is in fact the lowest bidder then they will most likely win the business. However, if the manufacturer has an opportunity to meet with executive management and explain how his system can make parts that will allow for new market opportunities, he at least has a fighting chance.

Let's say for example the more expensive system can produce a very precise angle cut. This opens up an opportunity to get into the knee replacement business. This new market might generate $500,000 in new revenue potential. If the more expense system cost an additional $50,000, one would assume this might make business sense. Again we are talking about value. This is the language executives speak. They understand the advantage of getting into additional markets that offer possibilities of higher margins. They are less concerned about the fact that their employees might have to learn how to operate a new piece of equipment. They are responsible for running a successful enterprise, so they have a different perspective in terms of evaluations of new products.

The message here is clear: as a professional sales executive, it is critical to sell at all levels. However, the message you deliver is not always the same. In fact it should never be the same. Tailor your sales call to the concerns of your audience. Additionally, it should not be a secret that you are calling on all levels. Senior management should know you are calling on various levels below them, and purchasing folks and technical individuals should also know you are calling above. It's a beautiful thing when you orchestrate a coordinated sales effort across your account.

It should be noted that it is not only important to sell at the senior level; it's equally important to have support for your product and company throughout an organization. For example, even though you might have a great business relationship with a VP or CIO, if that person retires, gets fired, or moves on to another position, your relationship at the account could be in jeopardy.

Tom, a very successful long-term account executive with EMC, related to me an example of how being single-threaded in an account can be detrimental. EMC had a fairly large presence at IMS in Pennsylvania. At the time there were two individuals at IMS who were primarily responsible for the evaluation and purchase of data storage. These two guys did not get along. In fact, according to Tom, it was much worse than that. Tom's relationship was very strong with the key person responsible for acquiring data storage, but he was somewhat hesitant to spend time and build a relationship with the other player because of the potential of impacting the relationship with his primary contact. So Tom continued to be single-threaded at IMS. He received the lion's share of their business, and IBM received the balance. It should be noted that the other contact in the account—the one Tom had no relationship with—was a big IBM supporter.

Then it happened: Tom's primary supporter in the account decided to retire. From that point forward, Tom's adversary, the guy who preferred IBM storage, was in total control of all data storage acquisitions. It was too late for Tom to affect change. From then on IMS purchased no EMC storage, and to this day it has been difficult for EMC to reestablish itself at the account.

Don't make the mistake of putting all your eggs in one basket. Make sure you socialize the value of your product or service throughout your account base. And make sure you do it at *all levels*.

One point I need to make is how overly abused the phrases "senior management will not approve this transaction" and "senior management never does business with any company other than XYZ" are. Anyone in corporate sales who has not heard these phrases uttered during a sales call has not been selling very long. They seem to be an easy way to dismiss a sales rep, especially when the prospect is not interested.

But who is senior management? Sometimes you get the impression there is a corner office in the penthouse with "Senior Management" on the door, but no one is ever in there. It's an elusive title that can be and is abused by many folks in an organization for various reasons.

The next time one of your prospects hides behind this term, ask him for a copy of the org chart. If he asks why you want it, say you're curious to see the box with "senior management" in it. Your point will be made. As they say in baseball, you won't know the players if you don't have a scorecard. The same is true in professional sales. Without an accurate organizational chart, it's impossible to launch a successful sales campaign.

In 1983, while representing Telex, I was working on an opportunity to sell personal computers to Noxell Corporation. Noxell is the company that manufactures Noxzema as well as the Cover Girl line of cosmetics. I had worked the account for three years and had a large number of displays and printers installed. Additionally, I had established very strong relationships with Jim, the VP of information technology, and several other folks in the IT department.

Jim was the final decision maker regarding any IT acquisitions. Noxell was exclusively using IBM personal computers at the time. My mission was to place an evaluation Telex PC at the account that would offer Noxell a less expensive alternative. The technical contact, as well as the individual who made the decision on PCs, was a fellow by the name of Roy. When I met with Roy, he seemed uninterested in taking a look at our PC offerings. There was no real reason, just a lack of interest.

One Thursday evening at the monthly DPMA meeting, I noticed that both Jim the VP and Roy the technical evaluator were in the room. They were both engaged in conversations with other folks while enjoying some pre-meeting cocktails. I walked up to Roy and started chatting. After a few minutes, I asked him if he would like to bring in one of our PCs on demo. I said there was absolutely no obligation—he could simply run some applications and see how it performed.

Roy had the response I mentioned above: "Senior management doesn't approve anything but IBM PCs. "

I asked Roy to sit tight for a few moments so I could track down Jim. I brought Jim over to Roy and then repeated what Roy had said: that Noxell senior management only approves IBM PCs.

Jim looked amazed and uttered the words I will never forget: "Who the F do you think senior management is? I'm senior management!"

The demo was installed the following week.

CHAPTER REVIEW

- Begin your campaign at the highest level in the organization.
- Get an accurate organizational chart.
- Continue to sell at all levels.
- Never be single-threaded in your accounts.
- Make sure all levels in the organization understand the value you bring to the table.
- Focus on business problems, not technical advantages.

CHAPTER 6

PRESENTATION SKILLS/PROPOSAL GENERATION

By far the biggest issue I hear from senior executives regarding presentations by sales folks is that they come prepared to present their *own* agendas. In other words if they have a thirty-five page PowerPoint presentation, they are hell bent on getting through each and every slide.

Many sales folks are under the impression that if they get through the entire preplanned presentation, they have made significant progress toward closing the sale. Somehow they feel that the presentation will answer all pertinent client questions as well as do all the necessary selling. How about the salesman who asks the audience to hold all questions until the end? Perhaps he has so much valuable material he's concerned a question might get him off track and he won't be able to finish in the allotted time. You certainly don't want your prospect to ask a question that might be pertinent to a sale, do you? I say this in jest. However, these are true stories I heard during the interview process.

If you are employed by a major corporation, you will undoubtedly be inundated by numerous presentations from corporate.

You will also be tempted to take one of these canned presentations and offer it without modification. Most major corporations have marketing departments they pay lots of money to develop sales support materials. Many of these presentations are outstanding. They most certainly can be used to assist in moving your sale forward. However, one should not assume that the *entire* slide deck is suitable for your client. There is no way a marketing specialist in headquarters can be aware of the specific issues and challenges of your prospect. The role of the marketing department is to provide the sales execs with effective support material. Your role as the professional sales exec is to determine which support material is relevant to your client. This means you might have to mix and match slides from several shows to craft a presentation that addresses your prospect's needs. It also might mean you have to create some of your own slides and insert them as well.

Let me be perfectly clear here: **EVERY SLIDE SHOULD BE PERTINENT TO THE ISSUE OR PROBLEM YOU ARE PROPOSING TO SOLVE.**

You should be able to make a key point with each and every slide you present. Each slide should have a specific purpose. This means you might reduce the number of slides in a given proposal significantly. For example the corporate slide deck for a particular product might be twenty-five slides. After you have finished deleting unnecessary slides and adding those that are more relevant, you may end up with a nine-page presentation. Your audience will applaud you for not wasting their time with corporate fluff.

Additionally, when you pare down the slide show you will be extremely comfortable discussing each slide. You will be able to articulate crisply the purpose of each slide and why it is relevant to the proposed solution.

Having a shorter and more relevant presentation also shows respect for your prospect's time. In today's corporate environment, people are extremely busy. When they're sitting in a presentation that is not specific to their issues or needs, they tend to get frustrated. Their minds wander, and sometimes they might even nod off.

It's important to understand that many times less means more. I've witnessed the most productive presentations where all the time and energy focused on only one slide. Let the prospect dictate which slides are the most relevant. Don't be in a hurry to move on because you are concerned about time. If you've come in with a very specific presentation and your audience is asking lots of pertinent questions, don't be concerned about getting through the entire presentation. This is a good thing—unless of course the questions are irrelevant and unrelated to the solution. In this case you will need to use your best judgment in order to get back on track.

On the other hand, if the questions are coming from the key decision maker or recommender then take whatever time is necessary to answer them. One would assume if they have lots of questions, they're serious about your product and company. Conversely, if you get through a forty-five-minute presentation and there are no questions, I would be very concerned.

The same respect for your client's time should be shown when you bring in another resource. If, for example you're bringing in a product specialist or senior manager to assist in moving your sale along, I recommend reviewing the presentation before it is given. Too many times these corporate guys or professional presenters have *their* slide shows. They've done them so many times they can do them in their sleep. They may be well-polished presentations, and he might be an excellent presenter, but if it's not specific to your account it will not be very effective. Ask to review it prior to the meeting. Make suggestions to pare it down and modify it to address your client's needs. It might be better to have a short presentation and spend the remaining time in discussion. It is *your* responsibility as the sales exec to articulate the mission to whatever resource you are bringing into your account. You *must* take sufficient time to bring these corporate resources up to speed so they can tailor the presentation (with your assistance) to be spot on. Don't make the mistake of bringing in a resource to present and have it backfire.

Now that we know not to waste our prospects' time with presentations that are not totally on point how do we prepare a compelling presentation? As simple as it sounds, it all goes back to doing more listening than speaking. Remember the statement "God gave us two ears and one mouth for a reason"? We all need to do more listening and less speaking. Read the chapter "The Art of Listening." If you become a skilled questioner and good listener, you will learn all you need to know regarding your prospects' issues and challenges. Having gained this knowledge, you have the pertinent data to formulate a compelling solution.

After spending the necessary time as well as doing the required research regarding how your product or service will address your prospect's challenges, you will be prepared to put your presentation together. Now you can go through the mountains of marketing material and select whatever is relevant to your client. As you can see, this takes work. It all starts with information. You can't possibly prepare a presentation that is specific to your client without this information.

But this is what separates the good salespeople from the great ones. The good ones take slide decks from corporate marketing and present them. The great ones do the work to make their presentations specific. When a client sees her sales exec has taken the time to fully understand her challenges, the sales exec is immediately viewed at a higher level. You gain trust and respect because of your desire to fully understand your client's environment. You are on your way from a sales rep to a trusted advisor.

I use PowerPoint as an example of a presentation that should be free of corporate fluff and spot on. The same is true for any presentation. It could be a whiteboard, a flip chart, a webinar, or a face-to-face sales call. The point is you don't want to waste your prospect's time! A fifteen-minute sales call that addresses the issues is far better than an hour-long meeting where you discuss how wonderful your company and products are.

Stay on point with the specific agenda you have crafted for the meeting or presentation. Most importantly you should have a very specific objective in mind. This might be modified based on how the presentation or meeting goes. However, you must have a goal in mind for those days' events. There are steps along the line to closing business. This meeting should be one of them. The steps could be as follows:

- **Get agreement that the solution is viable.**
- **Bring technical issues to closure.**
- **Discuss other clients that have the same or similar challenges.**
- **Review corporate strengths.**
- **Justify cost with ROI analysis.**
- **Deal with price objections.**
- **Maybe ask for an order.**

In any event, at the close of the session, you would ask the prospect if you met their expectations for the meeting or presentation. Before leaving you would make arrangements for your next step. A good sales exec would have a preconceived notion of what the next step would be.

When you get back to your office, send an e-mail to the folks in attendance. Briefly review what was accomplished that day and solidify what the next step will be. If there are still some unanswered questions, this would give your prospect an opportunity to respond in writing.

PROPOSAL GENERATION

A strong presentation begins with understanding the prospect's issues and challenges. The same is true for your final proposal. How can you prepare a compelling proposal without fully understanding how your product or service provides a solution? The answer is you can't! So do the homework to gather the necessary information. Much of this research most likely has been done already if you follow the guidelines above!

After many months of meetings, sales calls, and presentations, it is finally time to use the information you have gleaned to prepare a compelling proposal. In the same vein as presentation skills, it is your objective to prepare a spot on proposal that is not chock-full of boilerplate. The last thing you want to portray is that you inserted a few custom pages but the lion's share of the proposal is standard. You don't want your prospect to think you spent fifteen minutes preparing it!

In some cases your prospect will provide very specific guidelines for what they want to see in the proposal. They will actually give you the entire outline and ask that you fill in the blanks. This makes it easier to evaluate because each vendor is responding to the same questions and format. This is very common in federal, state, and local government procurements. Sometimes major corporations will follow this format as well. If this is the case, then you must adhere to the request. Having said this, it still is important to be very specific with your responses, and don't include lots of boilerplate just to make your proposal thick.

In most cases the prospect will leave the proposal's format up to you. Based on the numerous interviews I've conducted with executives, simple is better. In most cases executives are not going to take the time to read through voluminous proposals that go into extreme detail, particularly if the details are not pertinent to the solution.

Each chapter of your proposal should have a very specific purpose, and based on the meetings you've had with this prospect you should know which chapters warrant more detail. For example if you gleaned in a past meeting that your prospect had been burned by poor service, you might want to drive home the specific details of how your service is superior to the competition's. Include testimonials around your service proposition, and possibly offer a service response guarantee.

The key components of a proposal will vary by industry and product. However, there are certain areas that should be covered. Put yourself in the prospect's shoes for a second. If you were evaluating your product or service, what areas would you like to see covered? Below are the critical areas that should be addressed or included:

Executive summary
Company
The Solution
Service and Support
Investment Section (Pricing)
Return on Investment (ROI)
References and Testimonials

Executive summary-In my opinion this is the most important component of your proposal. It is akin to a lawyer's opening arguments in front of a jury. Spend as much time as necessary and seek out other opinions to make sure your executive summary is highly compelling. It should hit all the highlights of your proposal and entice your prospect to want to read the entire thing. There should be NO BOILERPLATE. The entire executive summary should be specific to your prospect and in no way be in a cut-and-paste format.

With the research you've completed in conjunction with the meetings you've conducted over the sales campaign, you should have enough data to write a specific executive summary that is spot on with your proposed solution. It should include highlights of the individual chapters of your proposal. It should touch on the value proposition of your solution, your corporate strength, your service and support, and the return on investment. In addition I would also highlight the value *you* bring to the table. If you have a history of supporting the account, work that in. If you're new to the account, describe your experience in supporting the account after the sale is made. Remember the person evaluating the proposal is interested in what happens *after* the sale! That is why it's critical to explain how you will make his life easier and make him look good if the business is awarded to your company. You, the professional sales exec, are a very important ingredient in the decision making process. Your strengths should absolutely be highlighted in the executive summary. As far as the prospect is concerned, *you* are the company.

Company overview-When writing your proposal, it's important to keep in mind that the company behind the product or service is very important. Many times a sales exec will minimize the company he represents and gloss over the company behind the product or service. This is a mistake. A wise decision maker knows the sales exec might not be on the account long term. He may make a decision to go with the proposal, and the sales exec may leave for another job opportunity shortly thereafter. It is therefore critical that your proposal includes information about the strength of the company in addition to managers and support personnel who would be able to step in if the sales exec were to leave the company. Of course much of this should have been covered during your sales campaign.

Additionally, the company overview section will vary depending on the competition. For example if yours is the largest supplier relative to the competition, you would present this as an advantage. If your company is a small player, you would emphasize the fact that you are nimble and can spin on a dime in order to get things done. Your proposal should also include financial information on your company that will comfort your prospect. Nobody wants to do business with a company that is on shaky financial ground.

The solution-This section should be very clear, and detailed enough to cover all questions. You want to spell out clearly why your solution makes the most business sense. From all of your previous meetings, it should be quite evident what the prospect's issues and challenges are. It is now time to put your solution in writing.

Start by defining the problem in as much detail as you can. This will assure the reader that you and your company understand the issue. Then clearly define your solution. Try to reference discussion points you have had with your prospect to reinforce your understanding of the issue and your solution. Start with the high-level issues and solutions and then dive deep into the details of how your company and products will address them. If this is a technical solution, it would be wise to have your technical team write this portion of the proposal. Then have other folks who are technical review it for accuracy. It is imperative that this be 100 percent accurate. If there is a question about accuracy, you stand the chance of the entire proposal being questioned.

This section should be detailed but still stay on point with the solution. This is not the time to discuss other products or services your company has that might be of value. If you honestly feel that other upgrades or products may offer value, then have another section dedicated to this. But don't comingle the solution with other products or services. It will just confuse the reader and has the potential to get them off point from what you are trying to accomplish.

If a major advantage of your company and proposal is the fact that you offer a whole host of other products that may be of value then have a separate section dedicated to this. You would also highlight this in the executive summary section as a major benefit of doing business with your company. However, the purpose of this proposal is to win the business that is currently on the table. Focus on that.

Service and support-Depending on the nature of your product or service, what happens *after* the sale can be the deciding factor in awarding the contract. If for example you are buying the same product from different vendors then service and support are most likely the determining factors. For example in the data storage industry, EMC storage can be purchased from a whole host of resellers. They are all authorized by EMC, but there is a huge difference in terms of service and support. The same is true when you purchase a new car. The decision to go with a particular dealer might have a lot to do with location, availability of loaner cars, service reputation, and price. The vehicle is identical.

It is your responsibility to understand how much value service and support play in your proposal and make certain they are fully addressed.

Investment section-This is a professional way of addressing pricing. We call it *investment* instead of cost. *Investments* sounds better than *pricing*, but the fact of the matter is this is the section that your prospect will most likely go to first. Everyone is curious about the price. If the executive summary is not too long, one would hope it would be read first.

In any event make your investment section crisp and clear. Don't make it difficult to understand. Offer a granular breakdown if possible. Offer itemized pricing to alleviate confusion. If there are discounts for large orders by all means make that clear. Be sure to provide the specific pricing that was asked for. If you have some other options you feel your prospect would find attractive, offer another page titled "Alternative Investment Options." But make sure to provide what the customer originally asked for first.

It's also important to label the page with your prospect's name on top. It should not appear generic in any way. This pricing is specific for your prospect.

Return on investment-It's difficult to provide generic advice in terms of ROI. The bottom line is you need to take the necessary time to cost-justify your proposal. Your proposal will either save your prospect money or make your prospect money. Those are the only options! So your job is to demonstrate in this section how that will be accomplished.

Your objective is to cost justify your proposal in the shortest period possible. No one is interested in a proposal that pays for itself in twenty years. In some cases your proposal can be cost justified by both saving money and making money. This was the case with EMC data storage. We could show how the storage would improve application performance and therefore result in increased profits. We could also reduce costs because of lower air conditioning and electrical consumption. In many cases a $500K investment could be cost justified in three years or fewer.

The ROI is something in which the CFO will be interested. Make it clear, accurate and believable. If presented effectively it could be the deciding factor in winning the business. Because, at the end of the day, if your prospect wants your product or service he will need to sell it to his superiors. Take the time to give him the ammunition to do it effectively.

References and testimonials–Most likely during your sales campaign you have mentioned other accounts that have endorsed your company and products. In your final proposal, you will want to document several accounts that have as close a solution in place as the one you are proposing. If your prospect is a hospital it would suit you well to have a strong hospital reference. If your prospect is a bank, you would want to have a strong bank reference. If you don't have a reference in the same line of business then just select a local account that is well respected.

Be sure to check with these references before you include them in your proposal. They should be willing to entertain a phone call or a site visit. If not then they are not strong references. It's also important not to wear out your welcome. Take care of your references! They are a valuable selling resource.

In summary your proposal should make it 100 percent clear that you and your company fully understand the specific business challenge your prospect is facing. Then every component of your proposal should address this challenge by demonstrating specifically how you will solve the problem. The size of the document is not nearly as important as the content. Don't waste the decision makers' time with information that is not relevant to your solution. Be specific and stay on point. Your prospects will appreciate it. Their time is valuable. Respect it!

CHAPTER REVIEW

- Understand your prospect's challenges *before* your presentation.
- Prepare your agenda to address the specific solution.
- Every slide should be relevant to your objective.
- Adjust your agenda/presentation based on client feedback.
- Don't be totally focused on completing your presentation at all costs.

- Try to avoid canned presentations and corporate boilerplate if possible.
- Stay on point with your solution (assuming client buy-in).
- Your proposal should be crisp, specific, and custom tailored to your client

CHAPTER 7

THE FINANCIAL SALE/HOW TO MANUFACTURE NEW OPPORTUNITIES

After nine years of selling IBM mainframe peripherals for Telex Computer Products, I decided to take an opportunity in the computer leasing business. To be honest I was getting a little bored at Telex and viewed computer leasing as a step up in terms of career sales executives.

In my nine years at Telex I had rubbed shoulders with several very successful leasing professionals. They leased both our products and competitive products to our customer base. Some folks had their own small leasing companies and others worked for the big guys such as COMDISCO and Greyhound.

Through an acquaintance I interviewed for a sales rep position with a company called Thomas Nationwide Computer Co. Since I had no previous leasing experience or financial background, I was not offered the job. Undeterred, I continued to pursue this opportunity after arranging a face-to-face interview with Paul, one of the three partners. Finally, after much persistence, Paul gave me the job. Thomas Nationwide was a medium-sized leasing company. As I recall they had about twelve sales folks nationwide. They focused on very large transactions and were recognized as one of the premier players in the leasing industry. At the time I felt very fortunate to have landed this opportunity.

The leasing business offered five advantages I felt would benefit a career salesperson.

1) I could leverage ALL of the relationships I had developed as a sales rep for Telex.
2) I could lease ALL types of computer equipment (not just the ones Telex manufactured).
3) I could buy and sell used IBM equipment since a big part of the leasing business is buying and selling used equipment.
4) I would develop financial skills, which I did not have.
5) My sales territory would be much larger.

The leasing/brokerage business back in the late '80s was fairly basic. Let's look at Blue Cross Blue Shield of Maryland as an example of a typical customer. They had a financial person at the time named Ralph. IT would tell Ralph that IBM was delivering a new mainframe computer in April. The price of the computer was $13 million. Blue Cross was receiving a national discount of 20 percent, meaning the cost to Thomas Nationwide would be $10.4 million.

Blue Cross wanted to lease the mainframe for thirty-six months. I called my market maker and my internal finance guy. My market maker would forecast the residual value — what the computer would be worth at the end of the thirty-six months — and the finance guy would tell me what the interest rate would be. The rate would be based on the credit rating of the account.

After these internal discussions we would go back to Blue Cross with a monthly lease rate. At the end of the lease term, Thomas Nationwide would own the mainframe. Back then IBM mainframes held their value fairly well. Additionally, since Blue Cross bought at a very deep discount, there was a reasonable chance the computer would still be worth 50 percent of its original list price value.

If there was a good chance Blue Cross would upgrade the computer during the initial lease term, that would factor into the rate. The reason is upgrades are typically very profitable and can't be shopped around.

When all these factors were put into the equation, the monthly lease price was quoted. Then came the fun part. Ralph would typically call the three finalists and tell them they were in the running for the deal. He would then ask for a best and final price. In light of the above example, let's say my monthly lease price was $218,000. Now it was my job to try to get Ralph to give me a hint as to how I stood. Depending on my relationship with him, this may or may not have been an easy task. Some folks are completely closed-mouthed about their quotes. Others will tell you exactly where you stand in the hope of driving the price down as low as possible. And, most importantly, since the critical component of the monthly lease is the residual value, you have the potential to lose money if you forecast it too high. As a veteran in the leasing business explained to me, you might be out of business if you do too many aggressive deals.

So think about it! If you are leasing a $10 million IBM mainframe for thirty-six months, should you really care who you're writing the check to? You certainly don't want to deal with a company that has legal issues or that has written a contract that's unfavorable for upgrades or lease termination. But the bottom line is the rate is the only thing that matters. So attempting to make a living with a playing field like this can be difficult.

This brings me to point of this chapter. The leasing business taught me to be creative. In order to be successful I couldn't just submit thirty-six or forty-eight month lease proposals on IBM equipment. Yes, there were times when I would win. But I had to augment my sales in more creative ways to maximize my revenue and commission.

How do you become creative? It all starts with asking questions and carefully listening to the answers. In other words instead of simply responding to what the client is asking you for (in this example a thirty-six month lease), begin to understand what is behind the need to lease an IBM mainframe for thirty-six

WHAT THEY DON'T TEACH YOU IN SALES SCHOOL

months. The client has a particular business need to fill, and he believes a $10 million lease is the solution. Maybe it is. However, until you truly understand what he's trying to accomplish, it is impossible to know if other possibilities exist that might be more cost effective. Allow me to give you another example of what I mean. And although this is from the computer industry, my hope is you can translate the concept to your business.

The first thing I would ask is what IBM mainframe is currently in use and why it will not handle the processing load over the next thirty-six months. Is it pure processing power, more I/O channels, additional internal memory, or some other issue? Once I understand the technical reason for needing a new mainframe, I want to know if the prospect owns his current mainframe. If it is leased, I want to know the lessor that owns it and when the current lease term expires. The current lessor would typically have a huge advantage on the new deal, and if it is close to termination, the lessor could offer incentives to the client that could be rolled into a new transaction.

Now we know the technical and financial components of the client's mainframe opportunity. Maybe the IBM salesman and the leasing company sales rep convinced the client a new IBM mainframe is the way to go. We can't know if that's the case until we dig deeper. In any event we are now prepared to go back to the office and work with the technical and financial folks to prepare an alternative proposal. In this example we might be able to bring in a used mainframe as a sublease from another client that might provide the horsepower for twenty-four months at a price of $150,000 per month. Then, in the twenty-fifth month, we could provide the same mainframe the client wants to lease for thirty-six months for a twelve-month term at $200,000 per month. The result would be a savings of $1.8 million over three years.

Essentially we are dealing with two commodities. One is the equipment and the other is financing. Both can be had from a variety of leasing and brokerage companies. So a creative salesman who has fostered a strong relationship with the client is typically the one who wins the deal.

Having to earn a living under these circumstances teaches you the value of the financial sale. Taking the time to position your transaction as either an operating lease or a capital lease can be critical in getting a deal done. Understanding the financial impact from the CFO's perspective can mean the difference between winning and losing a deal. It is *your* job to understand how the CFO will evaluate your proposal. This is particularly true of a very large transaction.

I highly recommend learning how to use the basic functions of an HP financial calculator. Learn how to calculate the present value of a lease stream. Learn how to figure out what a monthly payment would be based on the client's interest rate and purchase price. Learn how to structure a transaction that gets you the present value (PV) you need so the transaction will be reflected as an operating lease. An operating lease is not included on the company's balance sheet. This can be the difference between winning and losing a deal. In other words figure out what numbers work in the client's budget and then be creative with the payment stream. Remember, leases don't have to be the same amount for the entire lease term. Be creative!

I only spent three years in the computer leasing business. It was not as financially rewarding as I had originally predicted. But—and this is a big but—I learned the value of financial selling. I look back at it as a master's degree in how to generate additional revenue that might not be apparent to a sales rep without a financial background.

An example of how to be creative and *manufacture* a deal might look like this:

You have had several positive meetings with Gene, who makes all hardware decisions at Baltimore Life Insurance. You have done a masterful job of selling the many benefits of Memorex/Telex tape drives. Gene would like to replace his older technology tape with your product. He has one problem: there is *no* money in his budget to fund the transaction.

Many sales reps would make a note in their file to follow up with Gene in six to twelve months to see if funds have been approved for the transaction. I suggest another approach before assuming the deal is dead. As you have found in several chapters of this book, INFORMATION IS KEY. In this case it is the financial dispensation of the IBM tape equipment that is key to understand. Below are the areas that I would focus on:

- Monthly maintenance of the current tape system
- Depreciation schedule if the client owns, or lease payments if they lease
- Power and air conditioning monthly costs
- Technical requirements in terms of performance
- Physical constraints — do they need more space in the data center for growth?

Armed with this information, you can prepare a detailed proposal that hopefully will show that Baltimore Life could replace its current five-year-old IBM string of tape drives with brand new equipment for the same if not lower cost. The justification would look something like this:

New Memorex/Telex tape system: $150,000

Trade in value of IBM tape drives: $65,000

Current monthly maintenance: $2,650

Disposition of current IBM equipment: Owned and fully depreciated

Power and air conditioning monthly cost difference: $275

Total square feet saved: 40 square feet

Since the customer owns the tape drives, the costs associated with using them are related to maintenance and power consumption.

The first thing I would do is find a broker to purchase the client's current tape equipment. In this example a broker would pay $65,000. This leaves us a delta of $85,000 to make up. I know Baltimore Life pays IBM $2,650 per month to maintain the equipment. This is an ongoing cost that will not go down. In fact there is a strong possibility it will go up as the equipment ages. If the customer knows he has to pay IBM $2,650 per month (if not more) to maintain his five-year-old technology, then he should be willing to pay that same amount to Memorex/Telex for three years in order to get new technology. And that is *exactly* the question I would ask Gene: "If I can structure a transaction that would put new technology on your data center floor for what you are paying IBM in monthly maintenance, would you be interested?"

If we have done our job as sales folks then his answer would be yes. I would then structure a thirty-six month installment purchase agreement that would PV back to $85,000. This is the delta between what his trade-in equipment is worth and what we need to get for the new equipment. In this example the PV of $2,650 at 7 percent for thirty-six months is $86,342. The new tape system would offer a thirty-six month warranty, which would mean no monthly maintenance. Additionally, in my proposal I would highlight the additional power and floor space savings.

I could relate many stories similar to this one about Baltimore Life, where I *created* a deal where there appeared to be no opportunity. However, the purpose of this chapter is not to brag about my financial prowess but instead to get you to think about how *you* can be financially creative in your proposals. In many cases you are attempting to replace a competitive product with your product. The point is to understand all the financial considerations of the competitive product. You may want to consider being aggressive in terms of taking it out in order to position your product for long-term success.

The bottom line is there is a cost to the current supplier's product. Even though he may own it, there is a carrying cost associated with owning it. Figure out what that monthly cost is and begin to think outside of the box. Your customers and prospects will respect you for your creativity.

Also remember, don't give up too soon. Information is king! Use it to be creative.

Consider leasing as a tool-Depending on your prospect, leasing may or may not be an appropriate strategy. Some companies lease almost all the equipment they use. Other companies are 100 percent purchase. Others do a complicated lease versus purchase analysis to determine which financial strategy best suits their current environment.

It is your responsibility to understand the financial landscapes of your customers and prospects. For example your prospect may not be able to acquire your product because the capital budget for the year has been exhausted. While he loves your product and would recommend the acquisition, he is under the impression that there is no money in the capital budget. In this case it is worth asking him to check with the CFO to see if there is money in the expense budget. If the answer is yes, you might be able to structure an operating lease, which allows for off-balance-sheet financing. In other words the company does not have to capitalize the acquisition. There are certain accounting rules that need to be met in order to qualify for this tax treatment. The CFO would be able to tell you what your monthly payment would need to be on a twenty-four or thirty-six month lease based on the acquisition cost. You might be surprised by the new opportunities you uncover by understanding in detail how your prospect prefers to acquire product. You can then structure your proposals in a way that gets approved.

Subleasing-If your customer or prospect is currently in the twelfth month of a thirty-six month lease, you might assume there is no opportunity to replace that product with yours. This may not be the case if you think outside of the box and gather the pertinent financial data. In the IT industry back in the 1980s, subleasing was a way of life in the IBM mainframe arena. I see no reason why this concept can't be applied to any hard asset that has current value in the marketplace. With most high-priced equipment, whether it is medical imaging technology, cranes, specialty vehicles, or manufacturing tools, there are typically various types of users. For example Johns Hopkins Hospital is a tier-one user of the latest and greatest medical technology on the planet. If a new technology becomes available, that doesn't mean the system Hopkins is currently using has no value. In fact there may be hundreds of other hospitals or medical centers around the country that would love to have Hopkins' system.

So let's say Hopkins really wants to lease this new technology, but they have two major issues:

- They are twelve months into a thirty-six month lease on the current equipment
- They have a fixed monthly budget of $30,000 for this department's equipment

Since Hopkins owes twenty-four months at $30,000 per month, the PV of the remaining lease stream is roughly $651,000. The purchase price of the new equipment they would like to lease is $1,100,000. Bottom line is we have a total of $1,751,000 in obligation and new acquisition costs, and a $30,000 monthly budget to work with.

We know the current Hopkins technology is only twelve months old and has significant value to many other users. Since a sublease of the current system is critical to the sale of the new technology, it is incumbent upon the salesman to find a home for it. Now, I am not an expert on medical equipment. I would have to assume there are ways to locate potential users of almost-new technology. These second-tier users are probably more prevalent than tier-one users. Once these prospects are located you would find out who would pay the most on a monthly basis. Remember, you have a twenty-four month obligation remaining at $30,000 per month. If the prospect would cover the entire payment for the remaining term that would be outstanding.

Let's be more realistic and assume they will only pay $25,000 per month for twenty-four months. This would leave $89,000 in terms of PV dollars. We would then add the $89,000 short-fall to the new equipment cost of $1,100,000 for a new amount to finance: $1,189,000. Using the same 7 percent interest rate, the new monthly payment would be $36,500. Now, since the monthly budget is $30,000, we would increase the term to forty-eight months. This would result in a new monthly payment of $28,300.

It is also worth mentioning that lease payments do not have to be level. The only thing that matters is that the lease PVs back to the purchase price. For example if your prospect tells you they have no money available in the current year, you can structure a lease payment that doesn't begin until January 1 of the next year.

Let's say your client has approval to begin making lease payments in the amount of $25,000 for thirty-six months beginning on that date, but would prefer to have the equipment installed and in use on September 1. And you would also prefer to book the transaction in the current calendar year. You can offer the following alternative lease program:

Months 1-4: 0 payments

Months 5-36: $28,000

You would simply add the appropriate amount to the remaining thirty-two months' payments to make up for the shortfall of the zero payments for the first four months. An HP 12C financial calculator can do this for you in a snap. If the client has a fixed budget of $25,000 then you would simply add a few months to the term to make up the difference.

Another example would be a step lease. If a client has increasing budget flexibility in future years, you can structure a lease to take advantage of this. A typical step lease will look like this:

Months 1-12: $15,000

Months 13-24: $18,000

Months 25-36: $20,000

The present value of the lease stream is what matters. Be as creative as you need to be to meet the client's financial landscape.

Again, these are examples to get you to *think*. They may or may not be appropriate for your sales model. The idea is to be creative and *manufacture* transactions that are not apparent. As you can see, putting together creative transactions like this requires a bit of outside of the box thinking. But the payoffs can be significant!

CHAPTER REVIEW

- Understand the financial disposition of the products you are replacing.
- Find out *all* costs associated with the products.
- If no capital money is available, explore lease options.
- If your prospect sincerely wants your product, meet with the CFO to explore creative options.

CHAPTER 8

WORKING WITH SALES MANAGEMENT

As a professional sales executive, it is imperative to understand by what means your manager is compensated and evaluated. Just like you must understand your clients' landscapes, you must have a similar understanding of what motivates your manager.

If we use the three-legged stool example, you must do your best to make sure the stool is in balance. In order for *you* to be successful, both your manager and your clients should be happy. If they're not the result will be tension from one side or the other. So how do you achieve this balance?

Make it a point at the beginning of each year to sit down with your manager and let him know it is important to you not only to make quota but also to support him in a way that will maximize his success. Allow me to explain.

Depending on the organization you are working in, your manager might report to a divisional VP, a VP of sales, or, in a smaller company, maybe the CEO or owner. He has a compensation plan that might have various components other than straight revenue. For example he might be compensated on any of the following:

Gross profit
Renewals
Gross margin
Account retainment
Percent Increase in sales
Monthly/quarterly/annual sales
New account penetration
Specific product bonuses

In some cases he might have goals such as getting forecasts accurate and in on time, or attending a number of meetings with key decision makers. Remember, he has a boss who might be demanding. If you understand his challenges and assist him in reaching his goals (other than pure revenue), you will go to the top of the class.

Asking your manager to share this information shows that you have a genuine interest in his success. Hopefully the components of your manager's compensation plan are tied very closely to your plan. If this is the case, when you prepare your annual business plan you will most likely be in sync with your manger's objectives. However, there will be times when your manger and you will *not* be in sync. This can create tension if it's not handled properly.

For example, back in the late '90s and early 2000s, when I worked for EMC, the sales executives' bonuses were based on annual sales objectives. In other words if a large portion of your sales quota came toward the end of the year, the entire bonus was paid. However, sales managers, divisional managers, and regional managers were paid on quarterly objectives. You can imagine what would happen at the end of the quarter with such a system.

Let's say you have been working with an account for many years and are confident you will receive the PO around the middle of April. Your manager needs the deal to make his quarterly objective. He comes to you and asks if there is any way you can move the deal up a few weeks. Here is where the relationship with your manger is put to the test — and why I believe it is crucial for you both to be on the same page.

If you have a strong working relationship with your manager and he respects your ability to manage the account, you will have a conversation about the pros and cons of disturbing the natural path the order is taking. He will take your lead regarding what effect it will have on your client if you ask for a favor. Many times if you ask for a favor you will have to offer some incentive—in other words discount the transaction in order to bring it into the current quarter. The important fact is that you can have a valuable business discussion with your manager and jointly come to a conclusion on the path to take.

On the other hand, if you haven't fostered a strong working relationship with your manager, the discussion might go something like this: "Scott, we need to bring your April fifteenth deal into the current quarter. Set up a meeting with the CIO so I can get this deal done this month."

Now, don't get me wrong. Sometimes managers are pressured from above and so act out of character when it comes to closing deals before they are fully baked. This is where the professional sales exec needs to insulate his clients from a manager who has the potential to sabotage a strong business relationship. After all if you are a professional and have worked hard to foster a strong, trusting relationship with your client, you don't want to jeopardize it because of an overly aggressive manager.

In my personal experience I have been blessed to have only one manager in my entire thirty-year sales career who I had to keep out of my accounts. Not that I would lose business or jeopardize my relationships with my accounts, but because he added unnecessary stress and tension that I always had to clean up. After sales calls I would typically have to call up the account and make an excuse for him. This would create additional issues when he insisted on joining me on future sales calls. I knew my customers didn't respect him, and he added no value, so it didn't make any sense to take him a long.

By the way I was not the only sales exec who had this issue. Our entire district was at its wits' end with this guy. In fact at one sales meeting he stood up in front of the whole district and said, and I quote: "You all suck!" How's that for motivation?

Apparently we were not selling the product mix he was being goaled on, and this was his way of delivering the message. Talk about transparent. I suppose his manager had told him he sucked, and he was simply passing on the message.

Many times this manager would show up in the office not professionally dressed, and therefore not prepared to make customer calls. The morale around the office significantly deteriorated during his tenure, and many folks, including me, came close to leaving the company. EMC was a great organization with tremendous products and the best service in the industry. For the most part, the sales execs enjoyed their jobs and were well compensated. The question was: how could senior management allow this to happen?

This brings me to the whole point of the story: we all make certain assumptions and take things for granted. Months after this manager was fired, I was playing golf with John, who at the time was two levels above where the manager had been. John asked me how things were going, and I mentioned the fact that I'd come very close to quitting the company because of this individual's lack of management skills. Actually I said it a bit crasser than that. John was *very* disappointed that I hadn't brought this issue directly to him. In fact he was ticked off at me for allowing it to continue for as long as it did.

I learned a valuable lesson. Sales folks who have long track records of success and therefore strong customer relationships are a very valuable assets that should be protected. They are the lifeblood of the company as far as future business. At EMC, in the span of five years, several layers of sales management had been inserted between John and me. I did not have an interest in sales management, and John had progressed from district manager to regional vice president. EMC had experienced significant growth. Territories were shrinking and more and more sales folks were hired. John's original district went from Richmond, Virginia, to Philadelphia, Pennsylvania. Now that was a region with two additional sales managers between us.

There was very little value added by this additional layer of sales management. In fact, in my opinion, the farther away you get from the customer the more difficult it becomes to add value and justify your position. You become more of a report machine and less of a sales support individual. In light of this new management layer, this manager who'd been fired had been able to hide out for about a year. Since he had seasoned sales execs on his team, he'd succeeded in spite of himself. No rep, including myself, had given any thought to bringing his performance to the attention of his manager or to John. What's harder to replace? Six senior sales execs who are generating $80 million in revenue for a district, or a dysfunctional district manage? Enough said on this topic.

Let's assume you have a very professional and supportive sales manager. It is your responsibility as a sales exec to utilize him in order to maximize your productivity. First of all ask yourself a couple of questions:

1) What are my strengths and weaknesses?
2) What are my manager's strengths and weaknesses?

Below are some of the areas to consider regarding you and your manager's strengths and weaknesses:

- Presentation skills
- One-on-one sales skills
- Proposal generation skills
- Strategic account-management skills
- Customer relationships
- Internal relationships
- Strategic partner relationships
- Product or service knowledge
- Competitive information
- Knowledge of company history

Since we are not all blessed with strengths in all of these areas, it is your responsibility to determine how you can best maximize your manger's skill set to drive more revenue.

Before you begin to analyze how both you and your manager can best team up to win business, you first must understand your prospect. This book has a chapter dedicated to this discipline. After all how can you determine which skill sets you can leverage if you don't understand in detail how your product or service can solve your prospect's business problems?

Now you are ready to begin your sales campaign armed with detailed information on your prospect as well as insight into how your manager can assist you with his specific skills. Take the necessary time to put together a strategic plan *before* you meet with your manager. Set up a time to review your strategy with him. If you have done the necessary homework, this meeting will be very productive. You should get valuable input and support from him regarding your strategy. One would hope he would be delighted to take direction from you in terms of what role you need him to play. Remember, *you* are the quarterback here. *You* are determining the strategy. *You* are asking for assistance in the areas where he will provide value. This is *your* account. He is a resource that you are deploying in order to turn this prospect into a valued client.

For example if your manager has a deep understanding of how your product solved a significant business problem for another client in the same industry, you can ask him to share that story with a senior executive at your prospect at some stage of your selling cycle. *Think* about how your manager can add value.

Once you get buy-in from him on your strategy, it is important to keep him in the loop regarding your progress. This is crucial for two reasons. First and foremost you want him fully invested in the account. If he buys in to your strategy and you are both in sync, he should be as interested as you are in turning this prospect into a customer. He has taken a personal interest, and if you lose he also loses. Additionally, he is most likely discussing this prospect with his superiors and therefore has additional incentive to do everything possible to win the account. After all *he* will have some explaining to do if the transaction is lost. Second, if the deal is lost it will be very difficult to criticize you for losing the business if he was working in lockstep with you.

Don't be intimidated!

In my world of technology sales, we would have opportunities to present our sales forecasts to our managers on a quarterly basis. Many times our managers' manager would also attend these sessions. Sometimes we would present our forecasts just to them, and sometimes we would stand up in a hotel meeting room and present them to the entire district or region.

In either case the bottom line is you need to be prepared. If you are a true professional, you should know the answer to every question that might be thrown your way. After all you are the one who is facing the customer. You have done your due diligence and understand your prospects' challenges, and have crafted the optimal solutions. So questions about timelines, budgets, the decision making process, and your competitive advantage should roll off your tongue. At EMC we called these *drill downs*. If you weren't prepared you could look pretty foolish in front of your peers. If you were prepared it was an easy routine, and in many cases you received some valuable input from management.

CHAPTER REVIEW

- Convey to your sales manager that you are interested in helping him maximize his comp plan.
- Have regular strategy sessions for your key accounts.
- Ask for buy-in from your manager on your strategy.
- Ask for specific assistance in areas where your manager is strong and can add value.
- Keep sales management informed regarding your progress.
- Be the leader—the quarterback—in all discussions.

CHAPTER 9

SELECTION OF RESOURCES

What do I mean by *resources*? Simply put resources are *anything* you as a professional salesperson can tap in to order to support the sale. One of the biggest lessons I learned is to fully understand and utilize all the resources available to you. Sometimes they are made clear to you by management or in training. However, often it is up to you to seek out *other* resources that might not be outwardly apparent. In other words *you* must determine what is necessary to position your company for the best chance of success.

When I was young, first with Burroughs Corporation and later with Telex Computer Products, I convinced myself that if I reached out for help I was not a capable sales rep. I thought I didn't need any help. I was full of foolish confidence. When I look back at those early days, I have to laugh and, more importantly, dream about how much more successful I could have been if only I had been educated on the benefits of utilizing any and all resources available to me. Some companies do better jobs than others in terms of providing their reps with an array of sales resources.

Before we look at the specific resources that might be available, let's first take a step back to determine when and why we might choose them. After all if we choose to use resources that don't advance our sales then we have wasted time.

Throughout this book I talk about the importance of making a connection with your prospect. The basic connection is paramount to establishing trust and respect. Any resource you deploy in support of your sales efforts should build on this connection. In other words it should continue to add value to you and your company. If it doesn't then don't use it.

Conventional wisdom would assume that bringing in your sales manager to meet your prospect would add value and advance your sale. This, unfortunately, may not be the case, and *you* as the professional sales executive must determine if management will help or hurt your efforts. This can put you in a very precarious position, and your effectiveness in keeping certain folks out of your account will be directly proportional to the respect management has in you. Two illustrations from my sales career will help crystallize this issue.

Back in the late '80s, when I was in the computer leasing business, I was calling on Commercial Credit Corporation in Baltimore, Maryland. I had worked hard to develop a connection and a strong business relationship with Jeff, a mid-level financial manager who reported to Debra, a senior level executive who essentially made the final decisions. Jeff and I got along very well. We had gone golfing together and out to lunch several times, and had developed a relationship around more than business. I genuinely liked him, and I believe he felt the same way about me.

We had been working on several leasing opportunities over the course of six to eight months but had not finalized any business. The leasing business is essentially based on two factors:

1) Relationships
2) Monthly lease rates

Finally, after quoting many pieces of IBM equipment, Jeff informed me he was going to recommend Thomas Nationwide Computer, the company I represented, to Debra, his manager, for final approval. Furthermore he told me that once he made a recommendation it was basically a "rubber stamp" when it went to Debra for a signature. He did, however, say Debra did want to meet with me and my manager since this was the first time Thomas Nationwide and Commercial Credit were doing business. Jeff had sold Debra on the fact that this would not be a one-and-done deal and he felt Thomas Nationwide would be a strong leasing partner in the future. To this end I had prepared a master lease agreement as well as the supplement for the IBM communications controller that was to be our first lease.

Thomas Nationwide was based in New York. The company only had about fifteen sales folks in the entire country. I essentially reported to one of the three principles. Paul, the partner who had hired me, was not very enthusiastic about coming to Maryland to meet my prospect. At the time he had much bigger fish to fry. However, after I gave him the hard sell about how important this was to me and the fact that there would be significant follow-on business, he reluctantly agreed to go.

Paul arranged the meeting pretty much at his convenience and arrived in a limo, dressed in a $2,000 suit. He got out of the car with one of the early portable cell phones attached to his ear. If you remember the movie *Wall Street*, Gordon Gekko, played by Michael Douglas, had the same phone. They were extremely expensive, and only a chosen few had them.

I met Paul at his car and walked him to the elevator. I reiterated that this was a done deal and that Jeff and his manager wanted to meet him as more of a formality. Jeff met us at the elevator and ushered us into a very nice conference room overlooking the Baltimore skyline. Shortly after that his manager, Debra, walked in. Just as Jeff was about to make the introductions, Paul's cell phone rang. I assumed he would either cancel the call or pick it up and inform the caller he was in a meeting. But he did *not*. What happened instead was one of the most uncomfortable situations I have ever experienced in my entire life.

Paul began talking as if he were the only one in the room. Furthermore it was not an urgent call. It was not even a business call. It was clearly a personal call. He discussed upcoming weekend activities for ten minutes. Well, maybe it was five minutes or three minutes, but it felt like ten. Jeff looked at me in amazement, and all I could do was give him and Debra a look of disbelief. This was the first time I had met Debra, and I was feeling it might be my last.

Jeff had worked hard on my behalf to position Thomas Nationwide as a strategic partner. This was to be our initial meeting to exchange pleasantries and kick off the business relationship. Jeff and I were mortified by Paul's lack of respect. Finally he got off the phone, and I did my best to gloss over the situation and get on to business. Jeff then told Paul they had reviewed our master equipment lease and he wanted to make one small change. It was minimal, and being that Paul was an attorney I assumed he would read it and approve it, and by some stroke of luck we might be able to salvage the relationship.

But no, that was not the case. Paul informed my prospect that he no longer did contract work. He has attorneys on staff who handled those details. Essentially his attitude came across loud and clear—this was beneath him. He told me to send it up to New York and they would look at it the following week.

Shortly after this exchange, Paul left the building, and with him left any chance of our ever doing business with Commercial Credit. I did, of course, attempt to resurrect the deal, but the damage had clearly been done. Eight months of hard work down the tubes in a half hour!

Now, if I had known Paul would have such a cavalier attitude, I certainly would have done everything in my power to keep him out of the account. Since the customer had insisted, I'd brought him, though I'd been hesitant. However, in no way, shape, or form had I believed he would lay an egg like this.

Clearly this is an example of when a potential resource you would expect to advance your sale actually hurts—and in this case kills—any future opportunity.

Now let's look at another example of using a resource for the benefit of advancing your opportunity. In 1994 I was calling on T. Rowe Price in Baltimore. I had done business with T. Rowe since the mid-'80s with Telex Computer Products as well as Memorex/Telex. Now I was with EMC Corporation. We were attempting to position our premier data storage system at the account. Our flagship offering at the time was a Symmetrix 5500 . Hitachi Data Systems (HDS) and IBM were the storage vendors at the time.

I did have several long-term relationships at the account. I did not, however, have a relationship with their current CIO, a fellow by the name of Mike. I found out that our new VP of sales came from HP and had very strong business and personal relationships with Mike, the CIO at T. Rowe. They had done business together in Chicago at different stages of their careers.

I asked our VP, who was also named Mike, to contact Mike at T. Rowe to ask him to join a foursome at the EMC Golf Skills Challenge event outside of Washington, DC. I played in the foursome with the two Mikes and my primary contact at T. Rowe. Following the outing I arranged a meeting to put together a 5500 evaluation program. This one golf outing because of the connection factor of the two Mikes significantly accelerated the selling process at the account. Our VP had essentially opened the door, and it was now up to me to make it happen. And believe me I took full advantage of the opportunity.

There is no doubt in my mind that I would have done business with T. Rowe without deploying this resource, but the timetable would have been elongated. It is always beneficial to utilize every resource available to add value and accelerate your sales process.

We have just looked at two situations where sales management was deployed as a resource and the results were completely opposite. So how do you make a decision regarding the deployment of management? Do your best to determine if the resource you're considering will have a positive connection with your client. Obviously, if there has been a connection in the past, it will make sense (assuming it was a positive one), as was the case with my T. Rowe Price example. Maybe they worked for the same company in the past. Perhaps they both played college football. Maybe they are both involved in charitable work. Perhaps they're both huge golfers. Maybe they have similar personalities and are both from New York.

You get the point. It's up to you to determine some potential connection you can use in your meeting to make your client feel more at ease with your resource. Remember, people buy from folks they like, trust, and respect. You just need to start with *like*. Then you, as the professional, can determine who in your management chain would have the most favorable impact on your client.

If your supervisor insists on making the call with you and you feel she is not the best fit, then what do you do? Now you have the chance to show your professionalism, because if you have done your homework and truly understand what turns your client on and off, your can explain that to your supervisor. And if she is worth her salt, she will listen to you and allow another resource to be introduced. If she's not, hopefully she will at least do her best in the meeting to overcome the issues you have pointed out.

As a gross example of this, if your client has told you time and time again that he doesn't trust young guys who wear bowties, and that happens to be an exact description of your supervisor, hopefully he won't wear his bowtie to the meeting. You get the point!

Let's take a look at some other resources that might not be as obvious. If you're selling a technical item, like I did, it is essential to have a technical resource available to answer technical questions. Technical people like to talk to technical people. Additionally, even though your technical resource works for your company, she is not a salesperson and therefore has more credibility. Too many times I have witnessed a salesperson taking over a meeting when there is a technical representative in the room. The sales rep wants to show the prospect how much he knows and only defers to the technical representative when he can't answer a question. This not only shows lack of respect for his technical resource but also impacts the effectiveness of the meeting. Early on in my career I too felt compelled to do more talking. Later I understood the value of allowing other folks to do their jobs.

Let me explain. One would assume you brought in a technical resource to answer technical questions that you as the account rep are typically not able to answer. Or, if you know the answer, you cannot explain it to the detailed level that might be required. But you are surprised at the meeting. The client asks questions you are capable of answering without any technical assistance. You should still allow your resource to answer *all* of the questions that are technical-related. Why? Because your resource has more credibility! Your purpose in this meeting is to advance the sale, not to show off your technical prowess. Allow the technical person to do her job, and you do yours. I can assure you the same answer will have more impact and credibility when it comes from a technical person and not a sales rep. Additionally, it will enhance your relationship with your technical resource.

If you represent a product that is manufactured in the United States, it might make sense to do a plant tour along with an executive briefing. This was a very effective resource for me at EMC Corporation. I would spend an hour going through our manufacturing facilities with a prospect, to give them an opportunity to see firsthand the quality and testing that went into every one of our data storage systems. We then sat down in a conference room and had various executives and technical folks come in to talk about specific subjects in which our prospect was interested. The program was tailored to the prospect and was not a generic pitch.

If I could not convince my prospect to fly to corporate, I would bring corporate to him. In other words I would design an executive briefing specifically for my prospect's requirements and then fly in the necessary additional resources, such as regional folks who had specific experience in the prospect's line of business. In some cases I would do this briefing at a local hotel. This would get the prospect out of the office and away from potential distractions.

References are a very powerful resource. If deployed properly they offer a level of comfort to your prospect that is hard to duplicate. In my line of work I would always take a prospect to a current account to see the equipment and talk to the end user. As they say, there is no better salesperson than a happy customer. Use this resource to your benefit as often as you can, even if you have to take a long trip! Many times it will be worth the effort. If you can't make a personal visit then the next best thing is to arrange a phone call.

One of the most effective resources I used between 1985 and 1995 was the Baltimore chapter of the Data Processing

Management Association (DPMA, though the name has recently been changed to AITP). We had meetings on the third Thursday of the month about an hour from my house, so it typically made for a long evening. However, I can assure you it was well worth the effort. At any given meeting there were typically four or five of my customers as well as eight or nine prospects. I had the opportunity to sit and have dinner with these accounts as well as buy them drinks in the bar afterward. Essentially this meant I had the potential to make ten or twelve sales calls in an evening.

I tried not to do any heavy selling at these meetings but instead introduced my prospects to my current customers and then let them talk. It was a way to enhance my relationships with existing clients and to get to meet potential clients in a relaxed environment. Whatever business you are in, look into organizations that cater to your client base and *join them*. But I would not recommend you aggressively approach every prospect in the room and ask for an appointment. Instead I encourage you to establish relationships that are based on connections outside of business. Talk about things not directly related to selling your product or service.

Make going to these meetings a part of your overall business plan. Go about it slowly, and don't expect things to happen overnight. Over time your relationships will begin to blossom, and you will be given opportunities to do business. Again this is another resource to deploy as a professional salesperson who is in it for the long haul.

In general I believe *people* are your most valuable resource. The more you understand about the folks you're calling on, including their backgrounds and experience, the easier it will be to determine which resources can be deployed to advance your sales campaign. For example on my initial sales call I always asked how long the prospect had worked at the account and about other accounts where they had previously worked. I would do that because there is a strong possibility they may have worked at a company with which I was currently doing business. In my twenty-five years of selling in the Baltimore/Washington, DC area, it was quite common for folks to move around. Strong relationships are a valuable asset when a decision maker moves from one company to another.

In the early 1980s through the early 1990s, I did business with Joe, first at an account in Baltimore called Service Center, then at an account in Rockville called Standard Federal Savings, and finally at Coca-Cola Enterprises. We had established a strong working relationship, and he knew if he did business with me I would not let him down. Another example was Gene, whose situation was different. He ran the data center at Baltimore Life Insurance. We established a strong working relationship that turned into a personal relationship as well. Gene, however, stayed with Baltimore Life for most of his career, so I didn't have the opportunity to follow him to different accounts as I did with Joe. Gene had the distinction of doing business with me for more than twenty-five years. We did business when I was with Telex Computer Products, Thomas Nationwide Computer, Memorex/ Telex, and finally EMC Corporation.

An interesting aside to this is that Gene and Joe used to work together and were very good friends. We all attended the DPMA meetings on the third Thursday of the month, which helped foster our business and personal relationships. To this day we all keep in touch.

Another resource is your peers in sales. It goes without saying that you should all share information about how you won as well as why you may have lost business. But do you share information when a person who has buying influence accepts a position at another account? Even if the individual is leaving your sales territory, it is a good practice to give the rep who will be handling the account to which the contact moved a heads-up. Think about it: wouldn't it be nice to receive a call from your counterpart in New York to say a satisfied user of your product is relocating to your territory? Additionally, you learn he is a baseball fan, likes to play golf, and loves Chinese food. From a business standpoint, you learn he is very technical, likes detailed proposals, and does not shop around for the best price but instead expects outstanding service and support. The only place you would learn this information from would be the rep who called on him. Do you think this knowledge would accelerate your opportunity to do business?

In 1981 I received a call from Steve, whom I had worked with in New York for Telex Computer Products between 1978 and 1980. He informed me that Rich, one of his good customers, was relocating to Maryland and would be taking a job as the head of IT for Sinai Hospital. He said Rich was a big fan of our products, liked to be entertained, and especially enjoyed playing golf. At the time Sinai was not a Telex customer. Armed with this information it didn't take me long to arrange my first meeting with Rich. We then had several lunches and played golf. We installed some evaluation equipment and, as I recall, within sixty days had our first order. The account became a solid, long-term client for Telex — all accelerated by a single phone call from a peer in New York.

In summary, understand from both personal and business standpoints how best to connect with your prospect. You do this by observing and listening. If you are smart you will attempt to get some advance information on the individual you're calling on in order to accelerate the process. Then deploy any and all resources at your disposal that will augment that connection and therefore help advance your sale. Don't use the "one size fits all" approach to selling. Every situation is different, and every prospect is different.

CHAPTER REVIEW

- Which resources will add value to your sales campaign?
- What resource has the potential to derail your campaign?
- Which folks have logical connections to your account contacts?
- Reference selling within the industry is a powerful resource.
- Don't forget to leverage your peers (other sales reps) if appropriate.
- Be creative with your resource selection.

CHAPTER 10

THE BUSINESS RELATIONSHIP/ ENTERTAINMENT

The topics of business relationships and entertainment, in my opinion, go hand and hand. I say this because it is very difficult to develop a strong business relationship over an extended period of time without involving some sort of entertainment, which is a very broad term. Technically if you buy a client a cup of coffee, that fits the bill.

However, entertainment also involves anything from going to lunch at McDonald's to taking your client and his wife on a week-long vacation. In my experience it is not necessarily the expense of the entertainment but the connection value it provides. In other words if entertainment does not advance the business relationship then regardless of the cost it should not be deployed.

As an example, if your company has tickets to the NBA championship game, yet your prospect could care less about basketball, don't give him the tickets. If you do give him the tickets, always attempt to join your client at the event, where you'll then have the opportunity to advance your relationship. There are certainly times where you have two tickets to a game and your client would like to take his son. Let him, but then follow up with your client immediately after the event to confirm he and his son enjoyed themselves.

I can't overemphasize the point that when you use entertainment as a resource, you should never expect something in return. Your client or prospect should *never* feel that he needs to do business with you because you provide lunches, tickets, dinners, trips, etc. He should want to do business with you because you represent a quality product or service and he likes, trusts, and respects you as the representative of your company. Entertainment is simply a tool you deploy in order to foster your business relationship. It allows you to get to know your prospect or client on a deeper basis. Most times this cannot be accomplished in an office setting.

It has been my experience that *most* folks, not all, will refuse entertainment if they have no intention of doing business with you and your company. The reason is they don't want to invest the time and energy with vendors if they don't see a fit. Time is a valuable asset, and spending time with sales folks when there is no fit is frankly a waste of time. This is good news for you as a professional sales rep—if your prospect is accepting some form of entertainment then there is a reasonable chance he is open-minded about your offerings and wants to learn more. There are, of course, exceptions to any rule, as evidenced by my experience with JC Penney back in the late '70s.

I was a young, hard-working sales rep for Telex Computer Products in New York City. At the ripe old age of twenty-five, I was extremely excited to have the opportunity to represent a quality product that competed very favorably with IBM. One of my prospects that represented huge potential was JC Penney. They were headquartered In New York. If I was fortunate enough to establish a relationship with the key decision maker, I could begin to sell 3270 products nationwide.

At the time they were a very large IBM mainframe account and had ongoing requirements for our 3270 display terminals. Through several phone calls, I determined who the technical recommender was. This was the person who did product evaluations but did not make the final decisions. His name was Jim, he was in his early forties, and when I spoke to him on the phone I immediately invited him to lunch. When he accepted, I was elated. After all I was going to lunch with the key recommender of 3270 products at JC Penney.

We had a brief meeting in his office, and off we went to lunch. I asked Jim were he would like to eat, and he suggested a very nice restaurant near his office. Remember, this was Manhattan; there were literally hundreds of fine dining establishments within walking distance or a short cab ride. We sat down, and the waiter asked if we would like something to drink before we ordered. As I recall Jim ordered something like a scotch on the rocks. So, to be social, I had to have a cocktail as well.

Jim then ordered an appetizer to go along with his drink. I joined him, of course. He ordered a glass of wine along with his entrée. Not to be antisocial, I joined him. At that point I was thinking I had the best job on the planet. There I was, enjoying a cocktail, appetizers, and glass of wine with my main course at a fine restaurant in the city with a prospect from JC Penney! And Telex was picking up the tab. It couldn't get any better than that. I was positioning myself for huge commissions when JC Penney started purchasing.

After we finished lunch, Jim ordered some fancy dessert I can't recall. We then had a couple nice cups of coffee. Jim had Grand Marnier or sambuca with his. Suffice it to say the lunch tab was north of $50, and that was a lot of money back in 1978. And, I must point out, drinking at lunch back in the late '70s to early '80s was accepted. In fact it was quite common. So you might have needed a nap in the afternoon before you got back to work. Lunches also were much longer than an hour. In fact for a lunch like this it could have pushed two hours.

I was very excited about how this business relationship had progressed. I felt it was accelerating rapidly. Jim asked for some information about Telex's products, and we scheduled our next meeting. I thought, why not ask him to lunch again? We could discuss all we needed to over cocktails and a meal! That would have been much better than his office.

So we scheduled our second lunch at another establishment of his choosing. This lunch was very similar to our first. We had another expensive meal with plenty of alcohol to wash it down. I thought I was in fat city with this account. He really must have liked me. Things were progressing faster than I could have imagined.

Jim asked for more information. We set up another meeting. He suggested we do it over lunch. In fact there was no need to go to his office. We could meet in the lobby to save time. So that was what we did. We simply went to lunch. My objective was always to place a demo 3270 device at the prospect. This way they could see firsthand that it was 100 percent IBM plug compatible. They could also see the quality of the unit and the fact that the keyboard matched up exactly with the IBM model. Getting a demo installed was critical to any successful sale. In fact if you were not able to get your prospect to agree to a demo, it would be virtually impossible to make the sale.

Therefore I had asked Jim repeatedly to allow me to bring in a demo. In fact I proposed a no-obligation demo. Many times I would have the prospect sign a document that stated if the Telex unit performed equal to the IBM device, they would purchase X number of units. This made the demo more of a commitment than just an open-ended evaluation and confirmed that the prospect was serious about doing business with Telex. It also meant I would get some business if the unit performed as advertised. Even if it was only for a small quantity, it would be a start.

With JC Penney I was not asking for any commitment. I was only asking for them to take it in on evaluation. Jim pushed back. He said his boss had to get approval from corporate before any device other than IBM could be installed on their mainframe. There was some lengthy legal document that needed to be signed before I could deliver our demo. So I asked if I could bring in my regional manager to meet with his boss to help accelerate the process.

Jim informed me his boss was very busy and really didn't like to meet with vendors. He preferred to have Jim do that. It was his job responsibility. I tried repeatedly to set up a meeting with Jim's boss, but was unsuccessful. For months I waited for this document to surface that would allow us to install our demo.

There were multiple excuses surrounding the delay. However, Jim and I were still having nice lunches, and I held out hope that we would ultimately get approval to install our demo. I knew this was a very large account, and therefore there would be more red tape and approvals. I also knew the payoff could be great, so I accepted the situation at face value.

One day a very interesting thing happened. I was waiting in the lobby for Jim. We were having another one of our lavish lunches. While sitting there I overheard Jim talking on the phone, telling the person on the other end of the line that he was in the process of setting up his vendor lunches for the following week. Apparently he had every day covered but one. The tone of the conversation gave me the distinct impression that he took great pride in taking advantage of sales folks and using them for free lunches at fabulous restaurants. It seemed like a game or a challenge for him.

Needless to say when I heard this conversation I was devastated. I was one of the vendors he used for free lunches! Was I that naïve? Or was I overly optimistic or just plain stupid? Regardless, I felt violated, used, and abused, and quite frankly made a fool of. When we went to lunch that day, I had to force myself to be nice and not let on that I had overheard his conversation. Looking back I should have confronted him in a nice way about his vendor lunches instead of making believe I'd never heard anything.

From that day forward I avoided lunches with Jim. We met only in his office. And as you might surmise, it became difficult for me to get meetings with him. He seemed to be very busy during the workday but always had time to have lunch. The fact is I never got the demo installed and consequently never did any business with JC Penney. I did, however, learn a valuable lesson: there are leeches out there. Not many, but they exist. You as the professional sales executive must be aware when you are being taken advantage of. At this point in my sales career, I was overly optimistic and didn't have the skill set to know when I was being taken advantage of. Fortunately Jim is the exception, not the rule. Most folks don't operate like this, however a word to the wise is called for.

Getting back to relationship building as it relates to entertainment, from both the salesperson's point of view and the client's, it should be *genuine*. Said another way, in a perfect world, it should be a win-win situation — the client gets a "thank you" for doing business (or for the potential of business) and the vendor enhances his relationship with the client.

In my opinion the offer of some entertainment value that is premature can come off as disingenuous. Let's use an extreme case to illustrate my point. Say you are making an initial sales call on a major account. You've never met the prospect before. You have a very positive first meeting and arrange for a follow-up session. As you are leaving his office, you ask him if he would like to go to the Super Bowl with you. What do you think his reaction would be? Talk about trying to accelerate the sales process!

Quality entertainment is a process. First you need to build a connection with your prospect. You want him to feel comfortable with you as a person as well as a vendor. Then, when the relationship starts to mature, you can begin to add various types of outside-the-office entertainment. The type would be based on your clients' needs and desires. Below are examples of some entertainment options:

> Breakfast/lunch/dinner
> Baseball/football/basketball games
> Golf outings or professional golf events
> Theatre
> Skiing
> Auto races
> Fishing/hunting

Additionally, if it is possible to involve your clients' spouses, that typically goes a long way toward enhancing the business relationship. For example if you recently signed a large deal you might invite your primary contact and his spouse to join you and your spouse for dinner. Once the spouses get involved, you are taking your relationship to a new level. Of course your spouse needs to be supportive and complement you in your entertainment efforts. I was very fortunate to have a wife who was an excellent complement and always made my clients' spouses feel comfortable. Hopefully your spouse will do the same.

One of my former clients, Eduardo, who works for a large banking institution in Washington, DC, related to me a story that speaks volumes. It's about a salesperson who didn't understand the proper way to utilize entertainment.

This account was an EMC customer for many years. We had worked hard to gain their trust and had quite a large installed base of data storage. EMC had various models depending on the level of performance the customer required. This was a benefit to the client because all data did not require high performance, so for data that was not accessed very frequently there was no need to spend money on high performance. The account had purchased one of these lower-performing models and was very pleased with the decision. The model was a 3300.

A salesman from HDS, a competitor of EMC, was calling on Eduardo, who mentioned he had a 3300 installed. As soon as the salesman heard this he laughed out loud. He then proceeded to say something like, "I can't believe you guys bought that junk." According to Eduardo the salesman continued to make a joke out of the 3300 without letting him say a word. The salesman then turned to his technical guy and reiterated what a foolish decision Eduardo had made.

After all the laughing stopped Eduardo finally had a chance to say something. What he said was that he was fully aware of the performance limitations of the 3300. He then went on to say that the performance was perfect for the application it supported and that he and his staff were pleased with the purchase. Now the salesman knew he was in trouble and was attempting to backpedal. First of all, even if Eduardo made a bad decision, laughing at the client will *not* win you points. That goes without saying. It never ceases to amaze me how so-called sales professionals act.

After the dust settled and the salesperson was about to leave the account, you will not believe what he asked Eduardo: He invited him to a golf outing in South Carolina! This was priceless. First he insulted him and then he asked him to travel to South

Carolina to play golf. Not "I sincerely apologize for jumping to conclusions about the 3300" and "that laughing was completely unprofessional of me," or "what can I do to get our relationship back on track?"

Eduardo related another incident with a salesperson he'd met for the very first time. Afterward the salesman told him, "We need to go to dinner." No one *needs* to do anything. I hate the use of the word *need*. Additionally, in 99 percent of the cases, after your initial sales call it is premature to invite a prospect to dinner.

This is an excellent example of a sales rep attempting to entertain a client without making any connection first. In fact it is just the opposite. The rep is under some impression that dinner will help advance his sale. Even if the meeting went well, in my opinion this is way ahead of schedule. Dinner is completely different from lunch, which is in the middle of the work day. Dinner is after work hours. This means you are cutting into your prospect's valuable personal time. Most executives work long hours and value their time away from business activities. If you're taking someone to dinner, there is a strong chance some business will be discussed.

If you're at a more advanced stage of your business relationship, it may be appropriate to invite your client to dinner. Perhaps suggest that your manager and the prospect's manager come along. Or, as I mentioned earlier, you could invite the spouses. Dinner typically takes your business relationship to a higher level since most clients do not accept these invitations lightly. Again, it has to be done after your relationship has advanced to a certain level or the invitation may not be accepted.

In my case I used business dinners with and without spouses very effectively through the years. They are an excellent tool to advance your business relationship. One thing to keep in mind, though, is your alcohol consumption. Be extremely careful in this area. For example if your client doesn't drink, I highly suggest you keep your alcohol consumption to a minimum. You might want to limit yourself to one glass of wine with your steak. If your client is a heavy drinker that doesn't mean you should attempt to keep up with him. Use good judgment when it comes to drinking. We all tend to say things we might not say when alcohol is involved. Be mindful of this while entertaining. Once something comes out of your mouth it is similar to getting toothpaste out of a tube — you can't put it back!

Relationship building is a process, and it takes time. If you continue to deliver on your commitments and treat your clients the way you would like to be treated, you will continue to gain their trust and respect. By augmenting the business dealings with specific entertainment offerings, you will enjoy the benefits of mixing business with pleasure. Remember, one is not a substitute for the other. You can't overcome poor business skills and a lack of commitment with events and fancy meals. Entertainment is a tool to advance your business relationship. It does not replace a poorly performing product or a nonresponsive sales rep.

One of my mentors in the area of entertainment was a sales exec I worked with in New York in the late '70s. His name was Bill. He had a warm and engaging personality and a tremendous knack for developing close business relationships with his accounts. He was a master entertainer and made excellent use of his expense account. Bill would say in a joking way, "I always make three sales calls a day: breakfast, lunch, and dinner." He was an expert at mixing business with pleasure. I learned a lot from him.

If you talk to Bill today, he'll tell you he regrets not staying in contact with the folks he sold to and entertained over the last thirty years. They are your portfolio of business contacts you can reach out to as a professional sales exec. You never know at what account they may resurface. With today's technology it takes minimal time to keep the channels of communication alive. Just a few e-mails per year are all it takes to stay in contact with business associates. You spend a lot of time developing these relationships; don't allow them to die. Bill will tell you he loved his customers when they were buying from him, but once they were no longer customers he dropped them like hot potatoes. If he had to do it over again he wouldn't make this mistake.

CHAPTER REVIEW

- Never expect business in exchange for entertainment.
- Entertainment should be used to help solidify a trusting business relationship.
- Don't focus on business when you entertain (unless your client brings it up).
- Be careful not to advance entertainment options too early in your sales campaign.
- Don't assume you are making progress with your prospect because he accepts entertainment from you.
- Be genuine with your entertainment offerings.

CHAPTER 11

SALES EXECS DON'T CLOSE LARGE TRANSACTIONS/ CLIENTS BUY BECAUSE...?

There has been so much written on the art of closing a sale. This book is not about sales techniques, and therefore we will not discuss trial closes, the assumption close, the hard close, asking for the order, or any other methodologies. They all have been beat to death in numerous publications and discussed in sales training for ages.

In addition, do you really think a major corporation is going to make a half-million dollar purchase that is critical to the success of the organization because the salesman learned a strong closing technique? This book is not written for folks selling timeshares.

It is my firm belief that if you are a true professional, the natural result of your efforts will be the sale. In other words if you take the time to execute on the wisdom and knowledge assembled in this book, your prospect will be asking you how fast can you deliver. This is not a book that teaches shortcuts to making a sale. Remember, this is a marathon and not a sprint. This book *will* teach you how to be a professional. But a professional sales exec is not successful long term by taking shortcuts and fracturing relationships in order to get a quick order.

The topics covered in this book are based on years of wisdom from some of the most successful sales execs in their fields. They will all tell you it takes commitment and continued execution on a daily basis to produce consistent and long-term sales results. There are no free lunches out there!

If, on the other hand, you find yourself in a position where you constantly have to ask when the PO will arrive, there is a good chance you haven't addressed all your prospect's needs. Think about it: if a person has pain and you have a pain killer for sale, is it necessary to keep asking him when he would like the pain to stop? There may be other vendors that offer pain killers. It is your job to make the connection with your prospect and demonstrate how your pain killer will help him most effectively, fastest, and most efficiently. The fact remains—he wants a solution to the problem.

I think it is wise to explain why I am not spending a lot of time on closing the sale. This book is intended to assist folks in accelerating their careers as professional sales execs. Although there are certainly chapters of the book that will be useful for *all* sales folks, the primary targets are folks who are running sales territories. Typically, when one discusses closing techniques, it is directed at situations where if the sale is not consummated that day, your chances of making the sale are essentially over. For example in timeshare sales, statistics and history tell us if the prospect leaves the room and the sale is not complete, the chances of getting the deal done are dramatically reduced. In fact the chances are basically less than 10 percent. That is the reason time-share salespeople deploy all kinds of pressure tactics to get you to sign *that day*. Because if you leave they know there is a 90 percent chance they will lose the deal. This book is not focused on this type of sale.

In the IBM computer business that I worked in for almost thirty years, sales were not made by manipulative closing techniques. For example I did not ask T. Rowe Price, "Would you like your $1.5 million data storage system delivered on Tuesday or

Wednesday?" or, "What else do I need to do to get you to sign this order *today*?"

Large transactions that are critical to the success of a company are not decided by a manipulative sales technique. Decisions are made based on a compelling and well thought out proposal that addresses the client's needs. Additionally, the relationship of the sales exec in terms of trust and respect is a key ingredient. Executives are not making critical, long-term, multimillion-dollar decisions because of a salesman's ability to close. In fact in most cases a sales rep in our industry wouldn't have the opportunity to ask for the sale unless he was a legitimate player. I'm sure this is the case in many professional selling environments.

I received an extreme lesson in how *not* to close a sale back in 1977. I was working for Burroughs Corporation at the time. My sales manager, Joe, suggested I go on a closing sales call with Marty, a sales manager in training who had a few years of field sales under his belt. Marty was a bright guy with a strong technical background. He had been working on a mini-computer deal with this prospect for quite a while. Today he would ask for the order. I was simply along to witness the event.

Marty and the prospect talked about the merits of the Burroughs mini-computer at some length. It had been installed in a type of "try and buy" program. After the small talk, Marty opened his briefcase and presented the prospect with the contract. The prospect was a bit taken back by the document. Back then they were very thick. In fact, as I recall, there were about five carbon copies. You had to press very hard with your pen in order to penetrate all the carbons effectively.

So here was Marty's closing sales technique, and I quote: "We'd like to have your business today." The prospect was a bit shocked by the statement and basically said he was not ready to make an immediate commitment. So my sales mentor continued on with his closing technique. His next statement was, and I quote: "We want your business. We *need* your business." After this statement I honestly thought Marty was going to get on his knees and start begging.

This happened in 1977 and had such an impact on me that it seems like it happened yesterday. Needless to say Marty did not walk away with the order. But I walked away with a huge lesson learned: I would never, ever put myself in a position where I felt I needed to beg for an order. I had been sent on this call to learn how to close a deal. What I'd learned was how *not* to close a deal. I wonder if Marty is still using this technique.

So let's talk about *closing the sale in a professional manner*. This means working through all of the components of your proposal in a very deliberate and professional way, and seeking agreement on every step. For example if you address the technical aspects of your proposal in terms of how it solves the customer's problem, then address the ongoing support of your proposal along with references. Then discuss the price and return on investment, and finally the delivery and installation. Then the prospect might be asking you to prepare the contract.

In many cases, if you address all of the salient areas of your product or service in a professional manner, you are light years ahead of your competition. The reason is many sales folks like to take shortcuts. They are looking for the easy way out. They are asking for the order way in advance of when the client is prepared to make a decision. Don't be one of them. It is an insult to an executive.

As part of my research for this book, I interviewed sales folks from industries other than IT. One individual I interviewed has spent twenty-three years working for Capital Forest Products. This was his first sales job after graduating from college. He therefore learned the business from sales folks who had been working at Capital for several years. The company is a lumber broker. They are basically the middleman between the lumber mill and the end user.

I've talked in this book about the fact that being a salesperson is about as close to running your own business as you can get. Well, when you're a broker, that takes it to an even greater level. You are responsible for both the buy side (the supplier) and the sell side (the end user). You therefore have to establish relationships on both sides. You are the true middleman. You'd better know the market or you can get stuck with an overpriced product.

If the supplier is a lumber mill, the end user could be Home Depot, Lowes, a manufacturer of modular homes, or any other company that has a use for bulk lumber. Tom was taught early on in his career that the way to make money was to beat up the lumber mills for the best prices. His mentor said, "If they want $2.25 for a 2X4, offer them $1.80." Price was all that mattered — that was the way Tom was initially taught. And price was so important because the primary focus of Capital Forest Products was Home Depot and Lowes. Both were price shoppers. So in order to win business, they needed the lowest price. And the only way to give Home Depot the lowest price was to buy from the mills at the lowest price.

It seemed to make sense to Tom. However, when he continually went back to the mills for a better price, he started to insult some of the suppliers and, in some cases, if he offered too low a price they hung up the phone on him. This whole scenario, where price is the only thing that mattered, was starting to get old with Tom. He had been in the business for only a few years but didn't like the long-term prospect of operating like this for the rest of his career.

So he began to think outside of the box. Instead of continually beating up the mills over prices, what if he paid a premium? He would therefore be able to purchase as much lumber as he wanted from a quality supplier. He would not be competing with other lumber wholesalers that just want to buy on price. He liked this idea. The only problem was Home Depot and Lowes were price shoppers. *Quality* was not in their vocabulary.

Tom needed to find a new customer for the quality lumber he could source. He needed a customer that was not selling to the retail market. A customer that valued quality, service, and custom lengths. He found that market in the shed industry. Tom could offer consistently high-quality lumber that was custom cut to the clients' needs. The shed manufacturers were willing to pay a premium because they saved money by not having to cut as much lumber anymore. Additionally, they could depend on Tom for high-quality lumber, which produced better sheds. They also knew they could count on Tom to make deliveries on time.

There was an additional benefit of this shed industry: since Tom was establishing strong relationships with the mills, many of them would offer him exclusives on their products. In other words they would call Tom and offer him the first right of refusal on a truckload of lumber. They would give him a week or two to sell it before they would offer it to another lumber broker. This was not written into a contract but was more of a gentlemen's agreement. The mill would naturally prefer to deal with Tom than the many other brokers who wanted to buy on price.

Tom broke the original mold that had been taught to him early on in his career. He decided to establish strong relationships with the suppliers instead of having adversarial relationships. Since a broker is responsible for both the buy and sell sides of the deal, it certainly makes sense to have relationships on both sides.

We know in other industries that having the right product to sell many times makes your job much easier. Take a car dealer for example. When gas prices are skyrocketing, it is much easier to sell a hybrid or fuel-efficient vehicle than a gas-guzzling SUV. The supply side often makes the sell side easier.

Tom focused more on establishing strong relationships with quality lumber mills. In many cases he had exclusive rights to products that other brokers did not have access to. This outside of the box, creative thinking has paid huge dividends for Tom's business. I asked him if he negotiated an exclusive contract with these key mills. His answer was no. They essentially approached him because they valued the relationship he brought to the table. And he had the end-user relationships that allowed the mills to be successful.

So the title of this chapter is about closing the sale. Did Tom close the sale with the mills? Yes, he did! But it was not done in the traditional sense as a salesperson would view it. What Tom did was build relationships of trust and respect with the mills. He did not do this in a week or two. It took many years of hard work. It looks to me like the prospects—or in this case the suppliers—closed the deal because they realized the long-term benefits of doing business with Tom.

I like the idea of having the client ask you for the order. It's a lot more enjoyable and certainly less stressful. The fact of the matter is if you do your job right, the prospect will be coming to you. The question is: are you willing to make the long-term commitment, as Tom did?

Diane, a sales rep with EMC, related to me a creative way she demonstrated the quality of her product by deploying a prop to turn the table on her account. Back in early 1992, Diane was working on a significant transaction at Reynolds Metals in Richmond, Virginia. Reynolds had been a long-term customer of EMC. They had replaced IBM memory with EMC-compatible memory in their AS/400 systems with great success. They enjoyed the significant savings EMC offered as an alternative to standard IBM internal memory.

Diane was now positioning a disk drive proposal—a product called Harmonix—as an alternative to the standard IBM disk offering. Diane and her technical team worked for several months on the deal. Larry, the key decision maker at Reynolds, seemed to be comfortable with the technology. The EMC team had convinced him the product was solid and reliable, and would perform the same or equal to IBM. But there was one problem. Larry was pushing back hard on the price. Although the EMC disk was less expensive than IBM, he was of the opinion that it should be discounted even further. He essentially told Diane that unless EMC lowered the price, his business was going to IBM.

Diane and her systems engineer called a meeting to discuss the value of the EMC proposal. They arrived with two unexpected props: a box of Reynolds Wrap and a store-brand aluminum foil. They challenged Larry to demonstrate why any customer would pay 30 percent more for the Reynolds Wrap. The customer took a piece of foil from each box and proceeded to demonstrate how the Reynolds Wrap clung better to a bowl. Larry spent about a half hour attempting to show the superiority of the Reynolds product.

Diane and her engineer were totally enjoying the event. Larry was definitely struggling with the demo but at the same time seemed to be having fun attempting to show the quality difference. Most importantly Larry got the point Diane was making. Putting your customer in a salesperson's position in certain situations might be a way to turn the tables a bit. Perhaps they will understand there is a limit to how much you can discount. In Diane's case it proved to be a winning strategy. The sale was consummated in a unique and somewhat unusual way. No hard closing techniques!

One of my favorite and creative ways to finalize a transaction is related in the chapter "Thinking Outside of the Box" — the story of Steve, an office products sales rep, who won a large, multi-year order by utilizing two silver dollars.

CHAPTER REVIEW

- Closing a sale is the natural progression of events.
- Don't insult your prospect by asking for the order too early.
- Customers don't like to be sold to.
- Executives don't make mission-critical decisions because of sales techniques.
- Never beg for business!

CHAPTER 12

HANDLING A LOST SALE/ WHAT CAN YOU LEARN?

L et's face the facts: *no one* likes to lose a sale. Particularly a large one you've been working on for a very long time. One that has been on your sales forecast with a 90 percent probability of closing.

This chapter will focus on what you can and *should* learn from a lost sale and how to gain value from the loss. The purpose of this chapter is not to examine *why* you lost the business but instead how you can benefit from the loss. Other chapters will provide information on how we can avoid a loss before it occurs.

So let's set up the typical scenario:

You have been working on a very large transaction with one of your major accounts for several months. As a professional salesperson, you have put together a very compelling proposal. Additionally you have tested the water in terms of the price, the product benefits, and the business impact for your client. You've had your sales management involved as well as resources from corporate. In addition you've had assistance in developing the pricing structure and final proposal details.

Your company has had a fairly long history of doing business with this client. There have been some bumps and bruises along the way, but in general the business relationship has been a solid one. There are a few other vendors that provide competing products to this client, but your company is clearly the leading provider. You had been expecting a decision by the end of March, but things are starting to drag into April. You ask your primary contact when you can expect the decision.

Your contact tells you it is being reviewed by senior management. You are still optimistic about a favorable outcome because of your business relationship and track record, but since the deal is dragging you are starting to get a bit nervous. One of my sales managers from many years ago had a saying: "A deal that continues to drag on is like a dead fish—the longer it lingers, the more it smells." As a professional you continue to ask if there is any more information you can provide, or if can you bring in your manger to meet with their senior management. You know the drill. By this time you are starting to lose confidence in winning the business and are considering doing something out of the ordinary to pull them over to your side.

The feedback from your primary contact is not exactly what you have received in past transactions. This leads you to become concerned that he's holding back some information. Overall your gut tells you the business is going to another vendor. A feeling of helplessness overtakes you as you struggle for answers and try to figure out what you can do at this stage of the game.

Then it happens: you receive an e-mail from the account, informing you that the deal you had been working on for several months has gone to a competitor. There is no explanation, just a note indicating your company was not selected for this transaction. You feel a sense of betrayal. You have had a long business relationship with this account. In addition you are the primary supplier. It has been on your forecast as a lock. You probed for reasons why the deal was dragging and did not receive any concrete data that would have allowed you to restructure your proposal or adjust pricing. You feel empty inside and believe you are missing a piece of the puzzle. Desperation is taking hold, and you feel a need to lash out at your client.

You begin to pick up the phone to tell your client they have made a big mistake. Then you decide an e-mail would be better because you are concerned your emotions will get the best of you on a phone call. An e-mail will allow for a well thought out and pointed attack on this ridiculous decision they made. You want to copy several people at various levels of management so they will all be aware of how foolish the client's decision was. After all your primary contact and good friend will need ammunition to overturn this huge mistake.

As you type your e-mail, you are impressed by how articulate you are while throwing your client under the bus. You review the e-mail for one last time and are about to hit "send."

We've all been in these situations. It doesn't have to be in a professional sales environment. It could be that you receive a nasty e-mail from a friend or family member. The fact of the matter is we all need to take deep breaths and allow the dust to settle *before* we respond totally based on the emotions of the moment.

This chapter is all about what we can learn from the loss of a sale. I think it is fair to say it will be difficult to learn anything from this loss if we throw our client under the bus. In fact if we expect to do business with this client in the future it is critical that we preserve our relationships at all levels of the organization. It never ceases to amaze me how so-called professional salespeople will let their emotions get the better of them in the face of lost sales. They somehow feel good about getting these emotions off their chests.

But think for a moment about the consequences of allowing your emotions to get the better of you. Below I'll name just a few. The list could go on forever.

- *You will never know the real reason you lost the deal.*
- *Your account will lose total respect for you as a professional.*
- *All the years you spent developing relationships throughout the organization will be negated because of one emotional response.*
- *The chances of turning the deal around are gone forever.*

- *You make your primary contact look bad to senior management.*
- *You make it easy for your competitor to replace you as the primary supplier.*
- *You've lost the opportunity to improve your overall ability to be a better sales professional.*

So what should you do when you get news that you lost a deal you honestly believe you should have won? The first thing you should do is take total responsibility for the lost sale! Yes, instead of putting the blame on the client for his poor decision making, you take the high road and shoulder the blame for not advancing a proposal that met the client's needs and therefore separated you from the competition.

In other words what you might say to your client is something like this: "My responsibility as a professional salesperson is to understand your requirements clearly down to the last detail. Then I need to formulate a proposal that addresses these needs better than the competition does. Clearly I did not do that, and I apologize. I intend to do a better job of servicing you in the future. In order for me to improve my support of your account, I need to fully understand what components of my competitor's proposal met your needs better than mine. I'm not asking you to go into all the details of the winning proposal, only to point out the deficiencies of mine so I can make improvements in the future."

Essentially what you are telling your client is that you value the business relationship you have and you are sorry you didn't meet his needs on this particular transaction. You are putting his needs above yours. People respond favorably to this approach. You are taking full responsibility to do better in the future. Additionally, if this is executed properly, you are strengthening your business relationship as a result of a lost sale instead of sabotaging it by allowing your emotions to take control. Your credibility as a valued business partner just got a boost from the loss of a deal. Do you think all the other sales folks who were also competing for this same deal are taking this approach?

The most valuable commodity you have as a sales person is your account base. The last thing you ever want to do is ruin your business relationships. You work long and hard to develop trust and respect. Don't blow it because of one transaction.

After you call your customer and apologize for not meeting his needs, set up a time for a debrief on why you lost the deal. Go into his office or invite him to lunch. This is the second time your emotions should be in check. After all this is the first time you are sitting face to face with the client who did not award you the deal you had been working on for a long time. Naturally it will not be a very pleasant meeting for either of you. And keep in mind he may say some things that might not be very flattering to you or your company about why you were not chosen for this particular transaction.

However, the fact of the matter is *you* set up this meeting to understand clearly why you lost the business. It is your responsibility to lead the meeting in the most positive way possible. It is critical that it does not become confrontational! Nothing could be worse in terms of impacting your business relationship. In fact if your customer feels tension and senses your anger about this loss, you will not be able to accomplish your objectives:

- To learn what your competitor did to win the business.
- To strengthen your business relationship with this customer.
- To continue to be or to become the primary provider for this client.

When you and your client begin to review the details of the proposals, it will typically come down to a few key points such as:
- Price
- Features/functions
- Delivery
- Track record
- Comfort level
- Service

As you review these components, it will become evident which was the determining factor in why you lost the business. This is important in terms of your ongoing relationship with this client but also regarding your ability as a salesperson to win business at other accounts. After all if you lost a deal at this account because of a feature a competitor had and you didn't, it could certainly present an issue at other accounts where you will be competing against the same vendor.

Once you find out the specific reason you lost the business, ask in a nonconfrontational way if you would have won the deal had you tweaked your proposal to address this reason. Then shut your mouth and listen to the answer. It is my opinion that the response given will offer tremendous insight into your relationship with the account as well as your ability to win future business.

If the answer is genuine and there is little question in your mind that the client had a legitimate reason to do business with a competitor, hopefully you can make adjustments for future opportunities. If the answer is kind of vague and ingenuous, then you might not have the relationship you think you have, or maybe you need to start calling on other influential folks within the company. In any case you have gained valuable information from this debrief meeting. And, if it was executed properly, your credibility as a professional salesperson has been raised a notch.

Back in the late 1990s, I was involved in a very competitive RFP at Blue Cross Blue shield of the National Capital Area (now CareFirst). I was with EMC at the time. We were the primary supplier of data storage and had a strong relationship at all levels of the organization. Our primary competitors were IBM and HDS (Hitachi Data Systems).

EMC at that time had some very innovative software that allowed for replication of data that could be used for backup purposes. This feature, called Timefinder, gave us a significant advantage if a customer needed to create backups of critical data without taking the system offline. Blue Cross was using this capability on systems that were currently installed and wanted it on the new data storage for which they had just issued an RFP. We knew that both IBM and HDS were working on a Timefinder-like function that would offer this backup capability. To the best of our knowledge both competitors were many months away from delivering.

Shortly after the RFPs were opened and evaluated, we learned the deal had been awarded to HDS. I contacted Sam, my primary technical contact at Blue Cross, and scheduled a debrief meeting where I learned that HDS clearly had a lower price than EMC and therefore were awarded the RFP. We then reviewed the technical details of the HDS product.

HDS had represented in the RFP that they did in fact have a Timefinder-like functionality and therefore met the technical needs of Blue Cross. We were very skeptical that HDS had this feature currently available. However, I believed it was not in our best interest to call them liars. After all there was a possibility that our competitive intelligence group could have been wrong.

So what I did was tell Sam that to the best of our knowledge HDS did not have a Timefinder-like feature and we had not seen it installed and operational in any account worldwide. But the RFP said they had it, and Sam was going to proceed with the purchase from HDS. Needless to say I was not happy with the fact that we were losing a deal at one of my major accounts to a vendor that did not have the proven functionality my customer needed.

But I bit my tongue and simply suggested to Sam that he confirm that HDS did in fact have this feature and could deliver it at the same time the storage system was delivered. I also suggested he see a live demo of the feature before executing the contract. I told Sam that Blue Cross was a valued client, and in the event HDS could not deliver this feature, EMC would get our systems delivered and installed quickly to meet their internal timetable.

A week or so later, Sam called to inform me that HDS could not demonstrate their Timefinder-like functionality, and therefore EMC would be awarded the RFP. At that point it would have been real easy for me to say, "See? I told you so. These guys cannot be trusted!" But instead I simply asked Sam how he felt about the way he had been treated, and I let him vent. Apparently HDS had thought they could win with a low price and then deliver the feature in the future. They got exposed, and that fractured their trust at Blue Cross. EMC, on the other hand, improved our reputation as a valued vendor and positioned ourselves as the primary provider of data storage for Blue Cross going forward.

This story describes two distinct approaches to selling. One is to attempt to win every deal regardless of the potential long-term consequence of destroying your business relationship. The other — and I believe it is the correct approach — is to be open and honest about a potential shortfall of your proposal that might prevent your company from winning the business. Explain different solutions that solve the customer's problem in a positive way. Continue to seek solutions that are in the customer's best interest. If your company cannot meet the needs of your client, gracefully bow out of the transaction and position yourself as best you can for the next opportunity. In the end your client will respect you for your character and integrity.

Pat, an account rep with Memorex/Telex, related to me a story I believe we can all learn from.

Pat was a national account manager working a very large 3270 display deal at Xerox Corporation in Rochester, New York. He had been working this opportunity for quite a long time and was well positioned to win the deal. He had a large installed base and strong business relationships. Various levels of management had been brought in to establish the commitment Memorex/Telex had to Xerox, and the entire account team had been focusing on IBM as the primary competitor. All sales materials, discussions, and proposals were directed at beating IBM.

Then, to their surprise, Xerox awarded the deal to AT&T. The Memorex/Telex team was completely caught off-guard; after all AT&T was not considered a formidable competitor. They were fairly new in the industry and did not have an established track record. Additionally, they did not have many of the features and benefits the Memorex/Telex product offered. So how could Xerox select them?

After a debrief at the account, the real reason for their awarding the deal to AT&T was uncovered. It seemed AT&T was Xerox's second-largest customer. In other words Xerox sold thousands of copiers to AT&T. Give credit to the AT&T sales rep—he most likely used Xerox copiers in his office and did a bit of research to find out just how much money AT&T spent on their copiers. Then he orchestrated a phone call between some influential executives to leverage this ongoing business relationship.

I'm sure the message came down loud and clear to the individual making the 3270 decision. It was probably something like this: "Explain to me why the AT&T 3270 display will not suit our technical needs. If you can't give me a compelling reason then you need to purchase from AT&T."

At the end of the day it simply made good business sense. As Pat said to me, though, it would have been nice to know this fact during the proposal process. He then could have asked his primary technical contact if there were any chance of winning the deal. Who knows what would have happened? But one thing is for sure: the Xerox prospect would not have been on the sales forecast at an 80 percent close. Additionally, if there had been a particular critical feature Memorex/Telex had that AT&T didn't, it might have made a difference. Unlikely, but having this knowledge would have certainly set up more realistic expectations regarding the outcome.

Take a professional approach to a lost sale. Make it a learning experience that will make you a better salesperson in the future. Allow it to help you build upon your business relationship and not destroy it. And finally, stay in close contact with your customer after the sale is lost. You never know if the winning vendor will not be able to execute as promised, resulting in an opportunity for you to step in and ultimately win the business.

CHAPTER REVIEW

- Keep your emotions in check when you receive the bad news.
- Take full responsibility for the loss.
- Don't blame other people.
- Ask for a debrief in order to learn how to avoid a future loss.
- Make this a learning experience.
- Use it to build on your account relationship instead of destroying it.

CHAPTER 13

ACCOUNT MANAGEMENT/COMPETITION

In my humble opinion account management and competition go hand in hand. The reason I say this is once you are successful in getting your product or service sold and accepted, you move from an offensive to a defensive position. You just spent six months working your butt off to win the business. Now it is time to deliver, install, and implement your offering.

Regardless of the product or service you must deliver on the promises of your agreement. And guess what? Any competitor worth their salt will be watching to see if you foul up. So you are now playing defense to prevent your competitor from taking the deal away. If you forget that there are other competitors that want your clients' business, and you take your eye off the ball, then there is a good chance you will be replaced. The fact of the matter is you don't want all of your efforts to win business to go for naught because of your lack of account management skills.

Too many times I have seen sales reps move on to the next big deal once a contract is signed! They feel their job is done once the sale is complete. Maybe there is an installation team or a support system in place that is supposed to take over so you, the sales rep, can focus on new business. Regardless, if you're being compensated and expect to continue to do business with this account in the future, *you* had better be involved in the delivery of your proposal. Because if the deal goes south for whatever reason, so would your commission.

Additionally, if you want to position you and your company for future business, it is in your best interest to stay involved and make certain the account is satisfied. As part of my research I interviewed many high-level executives. One of the comments I heard regarding sales folks is that many show up only when there is a deal on the table. Is that how *you* want to be viewed?

After the sale is completed this is an excellent opportunity to solidify your business relationship. By staying in close touch, you gain respect and trust. You are no longer in a battle with a competitor for the business. Your client has no reason to play his cards close to his vest. He is now interested in the successful execution of the proposed solution.

Both you and your client should now be on the same page. You both want the proposal to be a win-win. During this critical period, take the necessary time to assure the delivery is on time, the installation team is prepared, and all commitments are fully delivered. Depending on the nature of your business, this could be an excellent time to uncover other opportunities for additional business. And since the basic transaction is complete, any add-ons typically will not have to go through as strict an evaluation and negotiation process as the base deal. For example there may be other components of your product offering that were not included in the original transaction. Once the installation and implementation are underway, opportunities to enhance the customer experience may surface. An additional feature that might add value can be offered. I certainly don't know your business so this is just food for thought.

The point is: don't go to sleep immediately following the signing of the contract. Take advantage of the transition from prospect to customer in order to keep the competitors out and enhance your relationship moving forward.

As a young salesman, I missed many opportunities to grow business in certain accounts. I felt my responsibility was to sell new accounts. While this is an admiral goal and extremely rewarding both financially and emotionally, it needs to be tempered by the long-term opportunities within your accounts. These are two distinct skill sets. For example while working for Telex Computer Products, I focused on positioning 3270-compatible display terminals in IBM mainframe accounts. I was a very young and aggressive sales rep. Consequently I made lots of sales calls and installed many demos. For the most part they worked perfectly, and I received orders.

Telex was one of three alternative suppliers at the time. So my job, as I saw it, was to convince the data processing manager that Telex had a viable alternative to the IBM 3270 display. Then I would deliver my demo on my luggage cart and install it myself. The installation was simple. It involved plugging in the power cord and attaching the coax cable. Even I could handle that. The account would then typically have several folks use the demo to make sure it worked as advertised and they felt comfortable with the keyboard.

We offered all the keyboard styles IBM did, so in theory there was no reason why someone would not accept the demo. The only reason some accounts would not purchase was because the IBM rep might have tried to put the fear of God in the data processing manager. He might have said our device might somehow corrupt the mainframe and bring the system down. Then, of course, the DP manager would lose his job for making a non-IBM decision.

Believe it or not there were some accounts that would not buy anything but IBM. They had very strong relationships with their IBM sales reps, and no competing products were allowed in their data centers. This is an excellent example of a sales rep that has mastered the skill of an account manager and knows how to play great defense!

I had not developed this skill set in the late 1970s. I would do the hard part. That is:

- Uncover the prospect (IBM mainframe account)
- Contact the decision maker (IBM data processing manager)
- Present the product offering and value proposition
- Arrange to install a demo 3270 device

- Demo the device
- Ask for the order
- Arrange for delivery and installation

Then I would be off to another IBM mainframe account to repeat the process.

At that time I had a very large territory that consisted of a large part of Manhattan and Long Island. The accounts I called on were household names: Citicorp, Michelin Tire, Con Edison, Pfizer, JC Penney, Macy's, ASCAP, and Holland America Lines, just to name a few. I even sold to the Watchtower Society in Brooklyn. The opportunities seemed endless, and that presented a major issue: I did not have the knowledge or experience to determine when I should cut back on my new account selling and focus on account management. I didn't have account-management skills and therefore continued to go after new business. So I had lots of accounts in terms of numbers, but few accounts had large quantities of our products. For some reason I felt that once I got a few devices installed, all I needed to do was wait for additional orders to come in. I basically felt the product would sell itself, and once the folks in IT began to use it, most future purchases would come my way!

Now, granted, I was twenty-five years old, and the extent of my formal training was basic sales skills at Burroughs Corp. So I really didn't know any better. What I did observe, however, when I attended sales meetings were stories of successful folks at Telex who had sold hundreds of displays and printers to major corporations in other territories. Many of these seasoned sales professionals had only a hand full of accounts, yet they generated significantly more revenue than I did. Additionally, they had auras about them that reminded me of senior-level executives.

Of course they were older than I was. Most of the reps at Telex were in their thirties and forties. They seemed to be at ease with their positions in life as professional sales executives. They had an air of confidence about them that I wanted. With some it had to do with age, and with some it had to do with knowledge and understanding. Unfortunately, many times, knowledge and understanding come with age.

If I had to net it out in terms of what separated these senior sales executives from Scott Dunkel in 1978, it would be two things:

- They knew which accounts in their territories had the most potential.
- They learned how to maximize the revenue opportunities in these accounts and prevent the competition from gaining a foothold.

Essentially they had mastered the art of where their most valuable asset—time—should be spent. They approached their territories much differently than I did. They had strategic approaches.

Conversely, my approach was to attempt to put a demo device in every IBM account within my territory. It didn't matter to me if the account was a very large user of IBM 3270 devices or not. That account was in my territory, and I felt an obligation to make a sales call. Also, it didn't matter if the account was unreceptive to an alternative to IBM products. I would continue to devote time and effort in an attempt to install a demo. In other words in the beginning it was my mission to make a call on every prospect in my territory. It sincerely bothered me not to try to sell to every prospect.

As a result of this approach, I spent a fair amount of time with accounts that would rarely buy any product that did not have an IBM label. And I spent a lot of time with accounts that did not have a lot of growth potential. To make matters worse, I didn't manage very effectively the accounts for which I did install products—even the ones that had growth potential. As mentioned earlier in this chapter, I was under the impression that if they liked my products they would simply send in orders. My responsibility was to get the first few pieces installed and then wait for the fax to light up with orders!

Enough said about poor account management. Let's focus on how you can avoid the mistakes I made back in the day.

You are assigned a sales territory and a quota. The territory has a total dollar value potential in terms of revenue. It is your responsibility to generate as much revenue as possible from it. You are obviously limited by the amount of time in the day, so there are only so many sales calls you can make. You'll want to spend your time in front of accounts wisely. In other words you'll want to be in front of decision makers who need or want your product as frequently as possible. I know I'm sounding like Captain Obvious, but we cannot lose sight of this important fact.

First and foremost is the big picture. Before you can focus on account management skills, you must determine which accounts you will call on. I don't know your particular industry. Only you can seek wise counsel and do your homework regarding which accounts in your territory offer the most potential. This chapter is to make you *think*, not to give you the answer.

Here are some guidelines I would use to make this determination with the products I represented:

- Size of installed base
- Growth potential
- History of use
- Is the account receptive to change?
- Can you demonstrate a major advantage of your product over the incumbent?
- Do you have any relationships within the account that you can leverage?
- Do you have service and delivery advantages?

Depending on the size of your territory, this process might take a while to complete. But in my opinion it is time well spent. Since time is your most precious asset, you want to make certain you are using it wisely. This means you only want to spend your selling time with prospects that you have vetted and therefore determined have significant potential for your product. Additionally, you've determined they have a history of being receptive to change. Most importantly, you feel your product offering has significant competitive advantages you can highlight.

In my situation at EMC, beginning in 1993 and ending in 2005, I went through various stages of this process. In the beginning my territory was very large. There were only three sales reps calling on mainframe accounts in the Baltimore/Washington, DC area. As I recall I had about twenty-five large accounts to call on. It was therefore extremely important to prioritize time in order to maximize potential.

One of the most difficult things for me to do back then was *not* work on particular accounts. For me to make a conscious decision not to attempt a sales campaign on a fairly large account was an extremely difficult pill to swallow. However there is only so much time in a day. You need to make a business decision as to where to spend your time. And hopefully, after careful consideration, you will make the correct decision.

As time progressed at EMC, it became unnecessary to look at my territory and determine where best to spend my valuable time. You see, as the company grew so did the sales force. In 1993 we had three reps in Baltimore/Washington, DC, and in 2005 we had about twenty. Since my territory had been whittled down to five total accounts, it became unnecessary to spend a lot of time determining who to call on, because the decision was made for me: We had very large quotas and very few accounts, and we did not have the opportunity to call on any new accounts. So essentially I had to make quota with the few accounts on my list.

I remember a funny story from back in those days. I had come home from work and was telling my wife, Jackie, that my quota had just been raised from $10 million to $12 million. My son, Bryan, asked, "I guess they gave you some more accounts then, Dad?"

To that I replied, "No! In fact they took one away."

Bryan said, "That doesn't seem fair."

Welcome to the world of corporate America. No one said it was fair.

EMC would look at what you did in 2004 and add 10 or 20 percent depending on what they thought you could do. There was no analysis of your territory to determine if an account bought enough storage for the next two years or if an account was in financial trouble and might not purchase anything. No. It was just, "Here is your number, and if you don't make it we will consider an adjustment next year. Providing you are still employed.

So now we have identified the specific accounts we will be calling on. For the purposes of this discussion we will assume you have products or services installed and your account is a satisfied customer. Whether you have only a few accounts like I did in my final years at EMC or have prospects in your territory you are attempting to sell to, as I did in New York in 1978, the principles are the same:

- **Maximize the revenue potential within the account.**
- **Keep the competition out.**

I'm sure you're reading this and saying, "Thanks again, Captain Obvious!" OK, so how do we do this? By continuing to add value as a supplier. We continually work on our business relationships in order to take them to the next level. Our objective is to transition from a vendor to a partner and eventually to a trusted advisor. People throw the term around all the time — "we are a business partner with such and such a company." If you're a true business partner, your client thinks of your company first when he needs to purchase a product or service you offer. He doesn't go to his list of suppliers and send out a bid or an RFP. He doesn't call you and say, "You need to sharpen your pencil on this deal." No, he values your relationship so much that whatever you continually bring to the table on a day-to-day basis far exceeds the few dollars he may save by going to another supplier.

You make it easy to do business and never let your client down. When there is a problem, you as the rep get involved personally and resolve it. You take full responsibility for any issues and don't finger point. Your client knows you will always have his back in the event there is an issue with anything related to your product offerings. In other words you will never make him look bad for doing business with you. This point cannot be overemphasized. The last thing your client wants to do is make excuses to his boss for doing business with you. Protect your primary contacts at all costs. They are your most valuable assets.

In most customer environments, you will have a primary sales contact. This is the person directly responsible for the evaluation and ordering of your product or service. There might be technical folks who report to her, or maybe a purchasing person who executes based on direction from your primary contact. Additionally, your primary contact reports to someone. For the purposes of this discussion the title is not relevant. The fact of the matter is, in order to protect your position as the valued partner; you must establish relationships with these other folks at your account.

Too many times sales reps get comfortable with their primary contacts. They're getting all the business. They might even have personal relationships. Therefore they are confident they will continue to win all the business based on these relationships. I can tell you from my own experience, as well as from my interviews with other sales professionals, it is never a good idea to be single-threaded at an account. It's important to establish relationships with the folks above and below your primary contact. Believe me, I've been there and done it. It's very easy to get comfortable when you're doing lots of business in an account. Your primary contact is telling you there is no need to talk to his manager. You're dealing with the guy who calls all the shots, and you're safe as long as you take care of him. Think about it: you are essentially putting all your eggs in one basket. This is not good account management. This is not good defense against the competition!

Spend time with the folks above and below your main contact. What happens if your primary contact gets fired? If he leaves for another opportunity? If he gets promoted? You get the picture. The time to establish working relationships with the folks above and below him is not when one of the above events happens. The time to do it is *before* then. You can accomplish this by inviting the whole team to lunch or dinner. The lower-level folks who report to your main contact will certainly appreciate this. Or maybe you can take them on some sort of outing, such as to play golf. The same concept holds true with your main contact's boss.

In addition maybe you can bring in someone from your company who can add some value. Perhaps someone from headquarters would be a good fit. The bottom line is you need to figure out a way to establish relationships at all levels of your account. Use whatever resources make sense, but make it happen!

When these meeting are arranged, there needs to be a purpose. They can't just be to say hello and thank everyone for the business. No, you need to come up with a plan that helps solidify the long-term business relationship. Think about how your product or service brings value to their company. Think about the specific benefits you offer and then try to show how they directly make their jobs easier. Perhaps you can show how your products or services directly affect the bottom line from a financial perspective. Try to show how your product makes them look good. In other words give them information they can share with other folks in the organization about why it makes sense to do business with your company. In fact they would be foolish to give the business to anyone else.

Your message should be consistent. However it certainly should be tweaked based on the audience. Your objective is to share the good news of your company continually at all levels. Everyone in management should be aware of the value your company brings. You might be pleasantly surprised by the additional business you receive as a result of expanding your sphere of influence.

In addition, as I talked about in another chapter, folks constantly move from one company to another. The more folks who know about you and your product at a particular client site, the better chance you may run into them at another account sometime in the future.

Equally important is the fact that if you have established relationships throughout the organization, it is unlikely you will be blindsided by a competitor. It is very difficult for a competitor to gain access to your account if you have all levels of management in sync with your value proposition. Remember, change is a pain in the neck for clients. It takes additional work and effort for them to change vendors. Typically there is a compelling reason to deviate from an incumbent. Don't give your clients any reason to consider changing.

But don't kid yourself either. The competition will continue to call on your client and market to your primary contact as well as other folks in the company. Sales folks are aggressive and will be persistent. They may not give up easily. So never assume you have the account locked up! Always strive to add value and continue to enhance your relationships throughout the account.

And the last thing you want to do is badmouth your competition. If you find out that either your main contact or someone else in the organization is talking to a competitor don't be offended. They are most likely just doing their jobs. Instead simply ask, "What do you believe the competition offers that I don't?" If you have a strong relationship you will get a direct answer. Many times they are just doing their jobs and seeing what is out in the market. They need to be able to respond to their management if asked.

Don't be afraid of the competition. Instead be confident and address any client questions that might come up, and reinforce the value you and your company continue to deliver on a daily basis. Don't tell your client they would be foolish to do business with your competitor. This would be a big mistake. Spend your time discussing the fact that you look forward to continuing the mutually beneficial relationship you've been developing through the years. Then ask what you can do to improve it. Always take the high road. Remember, you are in this for the long haul.

A great example of strong account management and how it relates to competition was described to me by a former colleague of mine at EMC. Tom, a senior account executive with EMC Corporation related a story that speaks volumes about client relationships.

The state of Delaware was a very happy EMC customer. Tom had developed a solid business relationship with Jim, the state's IS director. IBM, in an attempt to place a new data storage system at the account, made a bold offer. They told Jim they would replace an existing EMC 5500 with a brand new IBM system (code named Shark) with about 50 percent more capacity, and they would do this at *no charge*.

This seemed like a no-brainer to Jim. But before he told IBM to proceed, he first called Tom, his EMC rep, to explain the offer. Jim didn't want to blindside Tom, who told him that was a great deal for the state of Delaware and he should take advantage of it. Tom then contacted EMC headquarters. It was widely know that the EMC lab in Hopkinton, Massachusetts, was in need of an IBM Shark. EMC needed to have competitive storage products so they could do performance testing. The folks in corporate wanted the Shark that IBM was going to deliver to the state of Delaware, and they were willing to exchange it for a new 5700 storage system from EMC with the same capacity as the IBM offer.

Tom called Jim and told him the good news: Jim could swap his EMC 5500 for a new 5700 with 50 percent more capacity for no cost. He told Jim to accept the IBM Shark but not install it. EMC would pick it up and deliver a new 5700. So this was a win-win situation. EMC got a Shark for their lab, and the state of Delaware got a new EMC storage system with more capacity at no cost.

IBM, however, did not make out very well on the deal. In exchange for their new storage system, they received a previous-generation EMC model. And rumor had it that the IBM rep was terminated. You see, he didn't have a clause in the contract saying the Shark had to be installed and utilized. One would assume IBM learned from this and would not make this mistake in the future.

Clearly Tom had the stronger relationship. Jim felt compelled to call his EMC rep when faced with this attractive offer from IBM. These phone calls *never* happen unless you are more than a sales rep on the account. Tom was viewed as a valued partner. Jim did not want to fracture this relationship by blindsiding him with the IBM offer.

CHAPTER REVIEW

- Focus on the accounts that offer the highest revenue potential and fit your ideal customer profile.
- Don't go to sleep once you receive your order.
- Your competitor will be watching to make sure you deliver on your promises.
- Maximize the revenue potential in your installed accounts.
- Be mindful of the time spent on accounts that offer little or no returns.
- Avoid being single-threaded (having only one point of contact).

CHAPTER 14

THE SALES TRIANGLE/MANAGEMENT-SALES-CLIENTS, OR BALANCING THE THREE-LEGGED STOOL

Balancing the 3-Legged Stool

Customer

Sales Exec   Company

Let me explain what I mean by the sales triangle. In a perfect world the sales rep, his management, and the client should all be on the same page—all three in balance in terms of what the product or service will offer the client. The sale should be win-win-win. That is, the salesman should be happy, the sales management should be happy, and of course the client should be happy.

Since the client is the one in need of the product or service, it stands to reason that it is incumbent upon the sales rep and his management to make certain all three sides are in balance and singing from the same hymnal. The balance must start with the client—if they don't have a need for the product then this discussion is over.

So let's assume the client has a need for the product or service you represent. The sales rep is the quarterback for the client. It is his responsibility to fully understand the challenges the client has and how his product or service will address them. In other words what are the pain points? Or how can your product or service increase revenue? At the end of the day, you'd better be able to save the company money or increase revenue. Those are the only two ways to increase profits.

Your responsibility as a professional is to use the tools you've learned in this book to ferret out the business landscape. Then deploy your solution either to reduce cost or to increase revenue. This, of course, is sales 101.

The purpose of this chapter is to reinforce the importance of consistency from your point of view as the feet on the street up through your management chain. I understand that in some companies it might be more of a challenge than in others, but you, as a true professional, should strive to achieve this. As far as your client is concerned, *you* are the face of the company. When he provides you with valuable information that is relevant to his success as well as future business opportunities with your company, you should be taking good notes. At the end of the day, if your company is not addressing the needs of your clients then your company may not be in business next year.

So it goes without saying that it is *your* responsibility to make certain the information you receive from your clients is shared with your management. The professional sales exec must keep his first-line manager informed, and one would assume the first-line manager should keep her management informed as well. This is good business. And is very important! Think about it for a minute. If your prospect or customer is sharing with you a particular feature or function your competition offers, and he is telling you it is important to him and your company cannot respond, you want your entire management team on the same page as you and the client. That is what I refer to as *balance*.

Not having all the features and functions is by no means a showstopper in every case. A senior rep should be able to craft alternative solutions to address the client's needs. However, at times there will be situations where your company does not have any solution to your client's needs. It is absolutely critical to communicate this shortfall up the management chain. If it's done professionally, your management team will fully understand why you lost the business. And hopefully, if this was because of a major deficiency in the product offering, changes will be made to allow you to be more competitive in the future.

At EMC in the 1998-2000 timeframe, our company had shifted focus from IBM mainframe storage to open-systems storage. The market was exploding with demand for data storage across all computing platforms. EMC had offerings for all UNIX platforms from IBM, HP, and SUN. We were also moving into the Microsoft windows arena, which significantly opened up new revenue opportunities. As a company we began to lose focus on the product that had put us on the map: data storage for the IBM mainframe market. We didn't keep up with some of the connectivity features of the new IBM storage products. Additionally we were demanding a premium for our storage. In other words we charged more for a terabyte of storage if the client attached it to his mainframe as opposed to his UNIX system. Ninety-five percent of the product was the same. The only differences were the cabling and the software.

As a result we began to lose market share in the mainframe market we had previously dominated. I lost significant business in some major accounts. You can imagine how frustrating it is when your valued clients prefer to do business with you, but your management will not allow you to discount prices to address a lack of certain features.

At that time EMC had senior reps calling on the major accounts. We were all documenting our losses and screaming as loud as we could to management regarding our inability to compete in the mainframe market. Unfortunately our efforts seemed to fall on deaf ears. It took several years for EMC to wake up to the fact that the mainframe market was not dead and that demand for this platform would continue for many years. The demand would certainly not be as great as open systems and Windows, but certainly it would not go away.

From a sales rep's point of view, we were doing everything possible to rebalance the three-legged stool. We were receiving clear feedback from our clients regarding why we were losing business. We documented and raised the issues up the management flagpole. Eventually management responded, but in the meantime significant business was lost.

Equally important is making sure your sales manager — and anyone else for that matter — who makes a call with you is thoroughly updated on your client from a personal perspective. For example if your client is a big Redskins fan and your manager is a Cowboys fan from Dallas, and yesterday the Redskins lost a playoff game to the Cowboys, your manager needs to know not to come in beating his chest about it. This would not be good. Any pertinent information about your client that would be helpful should be shared to avoid such awkward situations. Conversely, if you know your manger and your client have something in common, that should be shared as well. This always makes for good small talk before the formal meeting begins.

Of course if the primary reason for meeting is to move the sale forward then you as the quarterback should set the agenda. You might handle a portion of the meeting, and your manager might handle a portion. But you must orchestrate how the meeting will unfold. And, most important, both of you must be in sync — in *balance* — in terms of the message you are delivering as well as the desired outcome. If you run to pick up your manger at the airport and he is on the phone all the way to the client location then the chances of having a meeting where you are both in sync with the outcome is significantly diminished. There are several examples of the sales rep and the manager *not* being in sync in this book.

At the end of the day it is your responsibility to make this happen. There should be *no* case where you and a manager make a call without the proper planning. If your manager tells you he will handle the entire call without any input from you then he has little respect for you as a professional. I would encourage you to find out why he believes the rep on the account has no valuable input.

Dave was a senior sales executive with EMC Corporation. When I say senior, I mean senior. At the time he had been in direct sales for about twenty-five years and had done a short stint in sales management with Memorex Corporation. Through the years Dave had established a strong business relationship with the executives at Tyco Corporation. He had done several million dollars in IBM mainframe compatible data storage. As mentioned in previous chapters, EMC developed, manufactured, and sold a product called Symmetrix, which replaced the data storage IBM offered.

There was a very large piece of business on the table that Dave was working hard on winning. At that time EMC was offering several software options in conjunction with data storage. Depending on client needs, these software options would offer significant benefits and eliminate the competition. It was therefore to the sales exec's benefit to determine if these software options would be of value.

The key, of course, was to understand the customer's environment and be able to relate the software offerings to specific client challenges. For example if a client had the need to mirror his data remotely for disaster recovery purposes, then a particular software offering that was unique to EMC would add significant value. There were a host of software offerings available, so it was the sales executive's responsibility to understand the client's IT landscape in conjunction with his strategic plans and to formulate a strategy and proposal to address these needs.

Based on Dave's relationship, he had done his homework and determined that no added software was needed for the transaction that was currently on the table. Again it was to the sales rep's advantage to ferret out all software possibilities. The reasons were twofold. First if the customer benefited from the unique software then the competition was essentially eliminated. And second, the software added revenue to the deal, which resulted in higher commissions and bonus. So, suffice it to say, the proposal did not include any software.

As a professional rep, Dave had explored all software options and determined this was a hardware-only deal. This meant price would play a significant role in determining who would win the deal. A meeting was set up with the chief information officer (CIO) of Tyco and his technical staff in order to bring the deal to closure. Dave invited his sales manager as well.

The purpose of the meeting was to come to terms on price. Dave had prepped his manager regarding the fact that this deal was hardware only, and that he should not bring up the topic of software. Dave had gone down the software path and knew that to broach that subject again at this stage would infuriate the client. After pleasantries were exchanged by all parties, the very first thing the sales manager mentioned to the CIO was that he noticed Dave's proposal did not include any software!

Dave sat there in absolute shock. He thought he misunderstood what had just come out of the manager's mouth. Then the manager continued: "Did you know EMC has more than forty software products? And I bet *you* can't name ten of them." He went on to describe how many IBM mainframe customers were utilizing EMC software to solve IT issues and how shocked he was that this proposal was for hardware only. As you can imagine, the client did not take this very well, and Dave was totally embarrassed and struggling with words to soften the blow. Had the sales manager listened to anything Dave had mentioned in advance of the meeting? It didn't seem so.

As a result of this lack of communication between the client, the salesman, and sales management (the three-legged stool), this deal was obviously lost. But, just as important, the relationship between Tyco and EMC was severely damaged. Sales execs spend many years developing trust and respect with their clients. It is absolutely unacceptable that many years of hard work can go down the drain when a salesman and a sales manager cannot be on the same page.

Let me ask you a question: at the end of the day, who knows more about the needs of the client? The salesman who lives day in and day out with the client? Or the sales manager who might visit the account a few times a year? If for some reason sales management does not believe the sales exec is doing his job, the time for a discussion is *not* in front of the customer! It should be done behind closed doors. In this example the sales manager paid no attention to the person who knew the most about the client's needs. He decided totally on his own that he knew better. He was not on the same page with the rep and proceeded to alienate the client. The results speak for themselves.

This *balance* goes beyond the sales rep and manager being in sync during the sales process. After the sale is complete the balancing act continues because your job is not done until the client is happy and pays for the product or service. Depending on the product you represent, there could be delivery issues, installation issues, or overall ongoing support challenges. Communication up through your management chain does not stop when the sale is closed. All components of the three-legged stool must continue to come into play after the sale is closed. In many cases your competition is watching closely to see if you falter. You've won the business; now make sure your entire team is up to speed on the delivery process. Keep in mind you are not just selling a product. You are selling a long-term business experience.

Take, for example, a restaurant. Is the food the only component of the dining experience? What about the location? What about the service? How about the parking? For most people the entire dining experience is taken into consideration when deciding to frequent a particular dining establishment. Let's say you're going to a highly recommended restaurant for the first time. You were told the food is superb and the prices are very reasonable. It sounds great, so you head off with your wife one Friday evening.

The first thing you realize is there is no close place to park, and the restaurant does not offer valet service. So you park a half mile away. You drop you wife off and you walk back to the restaurant in the rain. You have a reservation for 8:00. You arrive at 7:50 and are told there will be about a half-hour wait. You want to go to the bar for a drink, but it is too crowded. So you and your wife stand in a corner for about thirty-five minutes until your table is ready.

Once you sit down, you are anxious for your martini. But your waiter doesn't show up to greet you for another ten minutes. In fact you are not even sure who your waiter is. Finally he arrives and you order your drinks. They do not have the vodka you like. Your wife likes frozen margaritas. This restaurant does not serve them. So you both settle for alternative cocktails. You then order your meal. The waiter is not very friendly. In fact you get the feeling that he is doing you a favor by serving you. This is making you very uncomfortable.

The food takes about twenty-five minutes to arrive. Unfortunately it comes out wrong. The waiter misunderstood what you wanted, and he argues with you. He insists you ordered a New York strip but you know you ordered a fillet. At this point you are very hungry and don't want to wait for a new steak to arrive, so you accept the strip.

Your wife's lobster tails are perfect. She is delighted with the taste and the presentation. Although you ordered a fillet you are pleased with the New York strip. It is in fact one of the best steaks you've ever had at a restaurant. It takes ten minutes to get your check, and because it is now very late you have no time for dessert or coffee. Additionally, you are not looking forward to the half-mile walk in the rain back to your car.

This, of course, is a fictitious story. I use it to point out the fact that the food is not the only reason to frequent a restaurant. It should be the most important reason, but it is not the *only* reason. The entire dining experience determines whether you will make a return visit. In this case, even though the food was outstanding, you wouldn't want to deal with all the other negatives.

The same is true for a product or service you represent. The product is certainly central to your success. However, if you make it too painful for your clients to do business with you, they will look for alternatives. Unfortunately, in some cases where clients have little choice, the sales reps and sales management make it abundantly clear that they have no choice but to do business with you. This is unfortunate because if they had a more humble attitude they would be able to leverage the products you *have* to buy in order to sell you the products you don't have to purchase. Clients don't like to do business with a gun to their head.

It is my belief that the further the sales exec gets from senior management, the greater the risk of losing the balance. The reason is obvious. As an organization grows and various levels of sales management get inserted between the customer-facing sales exec and senior management, there is more risk of losing contact with reality. In other words the balance between what the customer needs and what senior management views as important can get lost in translation. Just as important, when multiple levels of sales management are added it becomes difficult if not impossible for each level to add value. And if a level of sales management does not add value then what is the point?

In the dot-com era, EMC experienced extreme growth as customers' needs to store data were exploding. In order to meet this demand, EMC hired more and more sales reps. Sales managers were challenged to fill slots. Many reps were promoted to managers before they were ready. We lost some great customer-facing reps who turned out to be not so great sales managers. It was, needless to say, a very challenging time for the company.

At one point, believe it or not, there were six levels of sales management between myself and the CEO. Now, if the function of the sales manager is to assist the sales exec in closing business as well as the ongoing support after the sale, how can all this management work effectively? The answer is it can't, and it didn't. New sales managers naturally would like to meet with the key accounts in their territories. Customers wanted to know why they had to make time to meet with new mangers who'd been inserted between the rep and the original sales manager. And since many of these managers had a difficult time gaining access to key accounts, they became concerned as to how they could show their management the value they brought to the table.

The result was more reporting. The mid-level sales mangers needed to show their involvement by massaging forecasts and sales reports and forwarding them up the chain. Additional sales meetings were also instituted so the second-level sales management could ask questions regarding the sales forecast. This put an additional burden on the customer-facing sales execs who were responsible for bringing in the business. Since more and more information was demanded as well as more meetings, it meant less time making customer calls.

During this unique period, we had less-experienced reps in customer-facing positions, folks being promoted who were ineffective and generated more meetings and paperwork, and, most importantly, additional levels of sales management that added no value in terms of closing business. This is an extreme case of an unbalanced and out of sync three-legged-stool. And I must say that EMC abandoned this model many years ago. But it does present an interesting topic for an MBA white paper.

In order to maintain a good balance between the customer, sales management, and the sales exec, the flatter the organization the better. Said another way, place some of your best folks in customer-facing sales positions. Allow them to run their territories like their own businesses. Hold them accountable for revenue, expenses, and gross margin. Allow them to work the territory long term so as to establish key relationships and trust within the accounts. If the correct sales execs are in place; the need for multiple levels of management is reduced significantly. If multiple levels of sales management are eliminated, the company can afford to pay sales reps commensurate with their productivity. And if the sales reps are compensated accordingly, there will be little turnover and consistent account relationships. Strong account relationships result in long-term business and fewer competitive threats.

For some companies this is a difficult concept to understand. They somehow don't place enough value on maintaining consistent relationships with their accounts. In addition they don't have career paths for sales execs who want to stay in the field.

This is unfortunate, for it's my belief that sales excellence should be rewarded. If the company you represent does not value sales reps, and you would like to make it a career, not a job in sales, then it is time to move on.

Another way of being out of balance is when you as the sales exec sell a product or service that is not what you thought it was. In other words, through no fault of your own you find yourself in an awkward position with your client because of a miscommunication of some kind. The product does not perform as advertised, and even though the sale has been made you have an unhappy client. And since your objective as a professional is to maintain strong relationships with your clients for the long term, this situation presents major challenges. If the client believes you deliberately deceived him, the chances of maintaining a business relationship are slim to none. You spend way too much time developing relationships to have them fractured because of a misunderstanding. Take the necessary time to make sure what you represent in the contract is what you will in fact deliver. Make sure you, your manager, and the client are all in *balance*.

I had a situation that caused me to lose the trust of one of my long-term accounts. At the time I was new to the computer leasing business. I had a very strong and personal relationship with Walter, the data processing manager at Random House in Westminster, Maryland. I had sold him a significant amount of IBM-compatible displays, printers, and controllers while working for Telex Computer Products. When I moved into the computer leasing business, I naturally called on Walter to see if Random House had any leasing needs. It turned out they were in the process of upgrading their IBM mainframe. Walter gave me all the necessary details in order for me to prepare a proposal.

It was a very complicated deal. It involved taking out and subleasing his existing IBM mainframe, which had about twelve months remaining on its lease term. We would then source a newer and faster mainframe that would give them the horsepower to meet their data-processing demands. So we had to find a home for his current mainframe computer to offset his remaining twelve-month lease obligation, and then find a faster mainframe to meet his needs and show him one monthly lease payment over thirty-six months.

I was working for Thomas Nationwide Computer at the time. We had an excellent broker on our staff who handled all the logistics and presented me with a final number. We quoted a price of $42,000 per month. It turned out we were the low bidder, and based on my relationship with Walter we were awarded the contract. I had the paperwork prepared by our legal guy in Long Island. It was a master equipment lease as well as schedule one, which would be the new IBM mainframe at $42,000 per month.

I was excited because this was a large transaction. It also would be great to get a master equipment lease in place at a major account like Random House. In the leasing business it typically takes a while to get a master in place because of all the legal review that is necessary. However, once the master is in place it is much easier to attach schedules to lease other products.

So the bottom line was they needed the mainframe fast. Both our legal and their legal had to muddle through the master lease in an accelerated fashion. We got it done in several days, and I had their VP, Richard, sign the docs. Shortly thereafter we shipped in the new mainframe and uninstalled the old one. Everything went fairly smoothly. The swap was done after hours on a Saturday evening, as to not impact service.

About a month after the installation, Walter called me. He had just been summoned to Richard's office to get his head handed to him for doing business with Scott Dunkel. The company had received their first invoice, and it wasn't for $42,000. Instead it was for $37,800. The lease clearly stated the thirty-six month lease was for $42,000.

Richard called our home office in Long Island to find an answer. What he found out was that the $37,800 was not the first of thirty-six monthly payments; instead it was a partial-month payment. Since the mainframe was installed and accepted on the third day of the month, the $37,800 represented rental of the mainframe for twenty-seven days. The lease would start on the first day of the month following the installation. The term for this rental is called *stub*, and the day of the month the installation takes place on determines the extent of the stub payment.

As a new sales rep in the business, I was not aware of this tactic. It turned out the stub payment was a major source of profit for leasing companies. When negotiating master equipment leases, many times clients overlooked the fact that the lease specifically stated the lease term would commence on the first day of the month following installation. Therefore any partial-month payments would not be considered part of the lease term. Obviously, if the computer was installed at the tail end of the month, this probably would not be an issue. But the fact that Random House was being charged almost a full month of rental infuriated Richard. He was disappointed that his legal team had not picked it up, and even more importantly he felt I should have informed them of this rental period.

I later learned that Thomas Nationwide would easily modify the agreement to have the lease officially start at installation. But if the client didn't ask, they left it the way it was. For the record I went back to my management and asked if we could start the lease at installation and therefore avoid this stub payment, and the answer I received was "absolutely no." So there I was in an *unbalanced* situation. I had a very upset client and no way of resolving the problem since my company would not budge. In addition Walter told me that Richard was putting all the blame on me. I was the rep and therefore responsible for the contract as well as not being able to resolve the dispute. Walter told me this was the last deal Random House would ever do with Scott Dunkel.

I'd spent six years developing a relationship with this account, and based on a single transaction all those years of hard work went down the drain. I was completely blackballed from the account. That was the reality of it!

So the lessons learned here are that no single transaction is worth fracturing a solid business relationship over, and make sure everyone is on the same page regarding specific details of the deal.

Inconsistencies in compensation can create an *unbalance* between the sales exec and sales management as well. For example it should be a win-win for both the manager and the sales rep when a transaction is closed. This seems like another Captain Obvious statement, but it was in fact not the case at EMC for a period of time. At EMC the sales managers received quarterly bonuses based on revenue. The sales execs were not compensated on a quarterly basis. We had annual objectives. Additionally, and more importantly for this discussion, we were compensated very handsomely for doing profitable business. Makes sense, right? If you sold a deal at a certain level, you would receive additional compensation. In other words there was a threshold price, and if you exceeded it you would receive a nice bonus for every dollar over it. For example if you sold a deal that's $20,000 over the threshold price you would receive a $2,000 bonus in addition to your normal commission. This incented the reps not to give the store away and to do their best to maintain the highest possible price.

As mentioned earlier, the sales managers were compensated on a quarterly basis—*all* the managers. So there could be four or five between the sales exec and the CEO who were all compensated on a quarterly basis. Then we had the executive VP of sales, his VP of sales for the Eastern region, the mid-Atlantic regional manager, the area manager, and the first-line district manager all on the same page. They were all trying to accelerate transactions from the second quarter to the first quarter so everyone would make their bonus.

The one who had the best chance of moving the transaction from month four to month three was the customer-facing sales exec. And he or she was *not* compensated on a quarterly basis. Talk about an unbalance! To exacerbate the matter, the account reps were told to discount transactions in order to give accounts the incentive to order in month three instead of month four. So here was the bottom line: the sales execs were asked to bring in deals a month earlier by discounting them to the point that they would lose their bonuses. The company was asking a rep to give up a potential $2,000 bonus so four or five managers up the line might have a good chance of making *their* bonuses. This can be especially disturbing when the rep who owns the relationship with the account is 100 percent confident the deal will get done in month four.

It's hard to convince me that significantly discounting transactions at quarter's end is a sound business principle. Giving up higher margin deals in order to bring them into an earlier quarter will catch up to you eventually. This practice became so common that many of our customers refused to sign deals unless absolutely necessary until quarter end. In my opinion we created this customer behavior by consistently offering incentives at quarter end. At some point this comes home to roost.

I point this out so you see as a professional sales exec; you should do your best to find out how your management is compensated. If there is a disconnect, the landscape is out of balance, and the sales reps and sales managers will not be in lockstep. I am certainly not saying you can force change. But pointing this out to management should be an eye-opener to them and give them something to think about. Modifying a comp plan to make it *balanced* for both sales and management should not be that difficult. The fact that you brought it to management's attention should be viewed in a positive light.

As we finish this chapter on the three-legged stool, it's important to keep in mind the areas that you can affect and the areas you can't. Many times you are dealt a difficult hand in terms of your customer base or general sales territory. You might even have a difficult sales manager or regional manager who is hard to deal with. Understand that you may not be able to change the environment or circumstances. Your sales territory, quota, comp plan, and sales management might be cast in stone. What you can change is the way you approach it. Remember, *you* are in charge of *you*. Be consistent and smart in terms of the way you approach your customers and prospects on a daily basis.

Also remember, building a successful sales territory is not a sprint but a marathon. The execution of your sales strategies should reflect this paradigm. Rome wasn't built in a day, and neither will your sales territory be. But if you deploy the principles outlined in this book on a consistent basis, it will pay off.

One of the major lessons I learned in my almost thirty years in sales is that it's very easy to remain positive as a sales rep when things are going very well. When you're ahead of quota and money is flowing in, it's very easy to walk around the office in a very positive light. This does not take much effort. True professionals are able to handle the valleys as well as the peaks in sales, and if you are in this business for any length of time there *will* be valleys.

A true professional is someone who can remain positive through the difficult times. This is what separates the real pros from the rest of the pack. They remain positive in the face of adversity and continue to execute their plans, for they are confident that their strategies, executed consistently, will bear fruit in the future. I have seen numerous examples of sales reps who have had huge years because of being in the right place at the right time. Often they thought they were better than they really were. In other words they were not very humble. They thought they were totally responsible for their success. They may have been recognized at sales conferences for blowing out their numbers. Perhaps they received awards for sales excellence. As a professional you must take things like this in stride.

Sales success is not an exact science. Things will be unfair from month to month and year to year. Some sales folks will get preferential treatment for one reason or the other. This is a fact of life! The same is true in any business or industry. The difference in sales is that a compensation package based on commission will many times result in income levels that are out of sync. In other words two reps with very similar work ethics and competence will at times have significantly different income levels. This is the reality of sales. If this is difficult for you to deal with then you'd better find another profession.

The good and the bad of sales is that your income is highly leveraged. This means you'd better get used to living on something less than your high-water mark. In other words, if you have a big year, don't assume next year will provide the same level of compensation. This is a trap that many people fall into.

They have big years in terms of commission, and they make the assumption that this will continue forever. This is a huge mistake!

I have witnessed this scenario more times than I care to remember. The only thing that is guaranteed in sales is that if you have a big year your quota will be raised. There is no assurance that your income level will continue to be the same in the next year. Consider it a windfall; don't spend like it's your standard. You will thank me for this advice. There is no need to go out and buy that BMW or Rolex watch to show the world how successful you are.

Success is built over many years! It is not a one — or two — year deal. Save and invest the excess funds, and continue to work and execute your plan. You never want to be in a position where you are a desperate sales rep. Such people do desperate things, and this does not bode well for building a successful long-term sales territory. Be smart with the financial resources you have earned. You will feel a lot less pressure when you don't have to close a deal to make your mortgage payment.

A consistent execution over a long period of time, keeping the three-legged stool in mind, will result in much success. When you, your sales management, and your client are all in *balance* you can't help but be successful. Remember, there are no short-cuts — except for reading books like this to gain wisdom and knowledge. Take advantage of all resources that will accelerate your career. In addition, talk with seasoned sales execs in your industry. Even successful reps outside of your industry can provide valuable input and wisdom to help you avoid common pitfalls. The school of hard knocks will ultimately get you there, but why not perform like a seasoned professional before you're in your mid-forties?

CHAPTER REVIEW

- Educate any resource who is accompanying you on the call objective, and make sure everyone is on the same page.
- A sales call is no time to debate issues with your management.
- Your offering includes much more than the product itself.
- Communicate valuable input from your clients up through senior management.
- Don't assume your income will be consistent—plan for leaner times.

CHAPTER 15

THINKING OUTSIDE THE BOX

This term means different things to different people. The way I view the phrase is this: *approaching a particular challenge in an unconventional way.*

In the numerous interviews I conducted for this book ,it became abundantly clear to me that the most successful sales folks think outside of the box as part of their normal business activities. They apply unconventional thinking in conjunction with proven traditional methodologies in order to maximize their efforts. By combining time-proven techniques with "outside the box" strategies, successful sales execs increase their opportunities significantly.

The purpose of this chapter is to get you to think differently about your approach to your prospects and existing clients. While it is important to learn from successful sales folks within your company and industry, sometimes seeking wisdom from other sales execs from completely different industries will offer nontraditional approaches you haven't considered. Don't rush to judgment and quickly dismiss ideas and strategies that seem outrageous on the surface. Just because you or other sales execs in your office haven't deployed them doesn't mean they don't have merit. This chapter will include many stories from very successful sales execs who have deployed unconventional ways of generating sales revenues.

I believe you can think outside of the box in two ways:

Internal pertains to what you can do from an internal or company perspective in order to be more productive. We all have a fixed amount of time. How we deploy this resource directly impacts our success. In other words the more quality meetings we have with prospects and clients, the more revenue we should generate. So any tool that the company offers or that you invest in has the potential to make you more productive.

External pertains to a unique way of approaching your prospects and clients. This includes strategies you deploy to separate you, your company, and your product from the competition. These can be in sales calls, presentations, pricing, or the formal proposal. They can also be an "outside the box" approach to engaging your senior management.

EXAMPLES OF INTERNAL STRATEGIES

Back in 1984 my sales territory was the state of Maryland, Washington, DC, and Northern Virginia. I averaged more than 30,000 business-travel miles per year. Needless to say I spent a lot of time in the car. And for the most part it was wasted time.

At the time the cellular phone industry was in its infancy. Cellular One had a pilot program in the Baltimore/Washington, DC area. I met with the Cellular One sales rep to price a phone system for my car. It was a hard-wired Motorola system with an antenna permanently mounted in the center of the trunk. The cost with installation was slightly more than $3,000 — a tremendous amount of money back then. But the fact of the matter was I needed to be on the phone an awful lot to make appointments. In addition I needed to be in contact with corporate to follow up on deliveries and various other activities. The bottom line was I needed to be on the phone a fair amount of time. And if I was driving to and from accounts, I couldn't be on the phone. So the opportunity to be able to make calls while driving was very enticing.

However, there was no way that my company was going to pay for a cellular phone. I therefore had to decide whether or not I could cost-justify the purchase on my own. Three thousand dollars is a lot of money. But 30,000 miles every year in the car without access to a phone is an awful lot of wasted time. It didn't take me long to figure out that the payback on this investment would come in less than a year. If I couldn't generate an additional $3,000 in commission in one year with this productivity tool, then shame on me.

This turned out to be the best productivity investment I could have made. It not only allowed me to make more appointments; it allowed me to inform customers that I was stuck in traffic and would be late. I've always been a stickler for being on time, and this tool allowed me to keep in touch when the Beltway was jammed.

After a few months of use, I wrote a cost justification for the business use of the cell phone. I was therefore able to highlight the business calls on my bill and submit them to TELEX for reimbursement. Today we take cell phone use for granted. We can't imagine not having access to a telephone for business or personal use. Back then I would really think twice before I made a personal call. I knew I couldn't expense it!

Another internal tool I deployed while working for TELEX was a local delivery service. The way we sold product many times was to install demo units. These could be displays or printers. In either case the salesman would typically run by his office and pick up a piece of equipment and deliver it to the prospect's data center. The prospect would then install the display or printer and have various folks stop by and use it. The demo period would typically last a week or two, during which the rep would drop by to make sure everything was working as advertised and to check on the progress of the evaluation.

As a new sales rep my responsibility was primarily to open new accounts. So I always had a lot of demos in the field. I was constantly picking up displays and printers from one account and moving them to another, and then back to the office after the demo was complete. This took up a fair amount of time, and unless I had interactions with the prospects there was no opportunity to sell. Thinking outside of the box, I found a local delivery service I could call on the spur of the moment to have them handle these tasks. This saved me a significant amount of time and therefore increased my productivity. I had the service invoice me directly. I paid them with a personal check and then put the invoice on my expense report, highlighting the account where I was doing the demo. It was also a lot more professional to have a service deliver the demo equipment than it was for me to drag the units through the lobby in my business suit.

One of the best examples of a "thinking outside the box" productivity tool is an assistant. In years past, sales folks had administrators to provide support services to make the sales exec more productive. Today, with corporate downsizing, sales execs, for the most part, are on their own when it comes to administrative tasks. And depending on the company you work for, these required tasks can be very time consuming.

I knew several successful sales execs who hired part-time administrative help. The objective was to free them up to do what they did best: *sell*. The more time you take away from selling activities, the less productive you will be. So if your company is burdening you with reports that can be offloaded to a part-time administrator, then you might consider it. One sales exec I knew paid a woman to go through his expense reports and commission statements with a fine-toothed comb and reconcile them. He was convinced that she more than made up the cost of hiring her with the lost money she found. He hated taking the time to reconcile the statement and therefore didn't do a complete job.

In my experience, sales folks many times don't have a knack for paperwork and don't enjoy it.

Productivity is the name of the game. If the time you free up by hiring an assistant allows you to generate commissions that total more than you're paying your admin, then it should be considered. And when you consider this is a legitimate tax deduction, it has the potential to make even more sense.

Are there any tools on the market that will aid your productivity? Maybe there are software products or industry lists that will help you identify legitimate prospects. Are there organizations you can join that will give you access to your target client base? Would a new computer make you more productive? Would taking a training class be of value? The point is to consider investing your money in order to position yourself better for a higher degree of success and to free yourself up to be able to make more sales calls. It's tough to be successful if you spend too much time in the office. As my first sales manager, Phil at Burroughs, would say as he walked around the room full of young salespeople, "Anybody buying from you in this office today?"

The message was clear. Get out of the office and into your territory!

EXAMPLES OF EXTERNAL STRATEGIES

Thinking outside of the box was precisely what Steve did back in the mid 1970s. After graduating from college, he took an entry-level sales job with Xerox Corporation. Xerox had a fabulous sales training program and was an extremely well-organized and well-run company. Xerox also had a dress code: business suit and white shirt, period. No exceptions.

Steve was quite successful and was on the fast track to management. At the time his father was a partner in an office supply business. One day his dad invited him to join his company. Steve was somewhat hesitant. He enjoyed the professional selling world at Xerox and saw a great future for himself there. However his dad was quite convincing and enticed Steve to leave Xerox and join his company.

Steve started at rock bottom—sweeping the floors, doing internal paperwork, and running all kinds of errands. Steve's dad finally gave him a chance to hit the field, to do what Xerox had trained him to do. That, of course, was to sell. His dad instructed him on how it was done, and he began calling on office managers and purchasing agents, selling pads, pens, paper clips, pencils, and various other office products. Gone was the business suit and white shirt. Back in those days, sales reps in the office products field wore more casual leisure suits.

Steve was not having a lot of fun. Additionally, he was not selling much product, and consequently his income dropped. One day his dad invited him to an office products show at a local hotel. Steve was not interested in attending, but his father insisted. Steve was getting ready to tell his father he was done with the office products business and was ready to go back to Xerox.

While at this show Steve's dad asked him what he observed. Steve responded, "I see a bunch of unprofessional guys in leisure suits handing out free samples of office products."

His father told him, "Son, that is your competition." The inference was, *you ought to be able to beat them!*

That statement completely changed the way Steve approached the business. He made the decision to change the landscape completely. Instead of calling on purchasing agents and office managers, Steve would put his business suit and white shirt back on and begin calling at the chief financial officer level. He knew CFOs were interested in saving money, so he developed a sales presentation that addressed that need. While all the other reps were busy selling small orders to lower-level people, Steve was securing large transactions based on volume discounts.

Additionally he offered guidance in terms of lower-cost items that provided the same functionality. This message resonated with the executives, and he separated himself from the hoards of competitors who were stuck in the mud with the purchasing agents and office managers. This approach was never done in the office products business. These items were pure commodity. The only thing that mattered was price and delivery, and low-level folks could make these small decisions. That was conventional wisdom. That was how *all* sales folks approached the business until Steve came along and completely changed the game.

Today Steve runs a very successful office products company where he employs many of the same "outside the box" strategies he did years ago. As he says, "After all, we're talking about selling pens and pencils. We'd better offer our clients a smarter way to purchase."

Steve was an "outside the box" thinker in terms of how to get a prospect's attention as well. Back in 1990 he represented a dealer cooperative that was a leader in the office products business. He had been working on a very large opportunity at a major health-care consortium (VHOA). In fact the sales campaign had been going on for almost a year! The winning vendor would be awarded a contract to supply more than one thousand facilities with office supplies over the next three to five years, totaling more than $25 million. Needless to say this was one of the biggest deals Steve had ever worked on. Office supply companies typically deal in significantly smaller transactions.

There were several companies vying for the bid. Over an almost twelve-month period, VHOA whittled the number of vendors down to two: Steve's company and his largest competitor. Steve had worked long and hard to get to this point and was extremely excited about the possibility of being awarded the contract.

VHOA's decision maker called Steve into his office to discuss his proposal. Steve thought the reason for the meeting was to tell him that he'd either won or lost the deal. Instead the decision maker told Steve he was completely on the fence regarding who should get the deal. He went on to say he was very comfortable with both companies, and this was in fact the most difficult decision he'd ever had to make. Steve sensed his dilemma and offered a method to break the tie. He told the decision maker to look for a FedEx envelope first thing in the morning. Steve said the package would offer a solution to this difficult decision.

When Steve got back to his office, he acquired two brand-new Susan B. Anthony silver dollars. He glued them together with heads facing both ways and placed them in the FedEx package with a note reading, "Flip this coin in order to determine the winner of the bid. If it comes up heads then my company wins."

Shortly after the package arrived, Steve received a call from the buyer, who said the package was the deciding factor. He was in awe of Steve's creativity and felt compelled to award his company the business.

One of the sales professionals I worked with at Memorex/Telex related a "thinking outside the box" story to me. Pat was the national accounts manager for Prudential, which was in the process of moving to a new office. In support of this move, they asked Memorex/ Telex to pick up, box, and move several hundred display units to the new facility. The units to be relocated were monochrome displays and had been installed for several years.

Pat was in the process of quoting a price for the move when he had a brainstorm: why not present a proposal to ship in all new color displays to the new facility instead of moving the old ones? As he formulated his proposal, he assembled the following details and facts:

- Total cost to box, ship, and reinstall existing display units
- Existing monochrome units were coming off warranty
- The trade-in value of the current units
- Increased user productivity with new color displays
- Warranty on new color displays
- Budget dollars available for the move
- Intangible benefits of having brand new displays at the new facility

When Pat presented the actual cost difference over a three-year period between moving the old units and replacing them with new color units, Prudential decided to order hundreds of brand new displays! The result was a huge order that had not been forecasted. It was a win-win for both Prudential and Memorex/Telex. The bottom line was Pat turned a non-revenue-moving contract into a very large sale. That is creative thinking. Pat crafted a way of diverting money from a relocation bucket to an equipment purchase bucket. If a company is committed to spending the money anyway, why not figure out a way to turn it into a sale?

In my chapter on financial selling, I explain this concept. If a company has budgeted money for maintenance, power and air conditioning, etc. for currently installed tape drives, why not show them a way to divert those same dollars to new technology? You're not asking for a company to commit new dollars. You're simply asking them to be better stewards of the money they are already spending.

Sometimes thinking outside of the box involves being confident enough to propose a very large transaction. This was an area I struggled with in my early days of selling. I had the crazy idea that only the very seasoned sales execs would be able to pull off huge deals. And that maybe a prospect would look at a twenty-something sales rep and laugh if he proposed a multimillion-dollar transaction.

I was in my mid-twenties when I asked a very successful senior rep at Telex to make a call with me. Dennis was in his early forties at the time. He was heading our federal government sales efforts. In addition he had run several small businesses and was a very seasoned professional, and he wasn't afraid to spend his own money to improve his productivity. To this point he'd had a mobile telephone installed in his car. This was 1981, so mobile phones were not cellular. He actually had to radio a mobile operator who then had to call the number Dennis gave her. The connection sounded more like a CB than a phone. It did, however, serve the purpose.

The primary reason I asked Dennis to join me was this sales call was related to disk drives. The technical term was DASD (direct access storage device). At that time Telex was shifting focus from tape and disk drives sales to 3270 display sales. All of the new reps and most of the current reps had put the disk drive offering on the back burner. Telex did not have a good reputation in the market and there was plenty of competition.

Dennis was very technical in addition to being an excellent sales rep. I needed him more for his technical ability since at the time I didn't know what a disk drive looked like. He graciously joined me and gave me a true taste of how a professional handles a call. I say he joined me, but the fact of the matter was he handled the entire call. I watched and took notes. He had the ability to have a genuine interaction with the prospect in order to gather the necessary data for our proposal. He asked lots of questions and was a keen listener. Additionally, he had the ability to convey genuine interest in solving the client's problems.

But what *really* struck me was our debrief after the call. The reason for the call had been to replace a string of disk drives. As I recall the account had a total of four strings of disk. When we got back to the office, Dennis worked up a proposal to replace *all* of the disk drives in the data center! He had gathered the necessary financial data in order to present a proposal to replace all the client's existing DASD with Telex DASD. So he had taken a $150,000 deal to one close to $600,000! His point was, "Why not? It's worth a shot. The customer can only say no." Dennis exuded confidence. I learned a lot from him that day. Why not shoot for the big one? It takes the same effort as shooting for the small one.

In 1985 I took this "thinking outside the box" mentality to new heights. I had been working a very large 3270 display deal with the Washington Hospital Center. We had several displays and printers installed in nursing units during the evaluation/proposal process. One afternoon I was at the hospital, making a call on Bob, the operations manager. I had been having severe stomach pains for a few days but kept brushing them off as something that would go away. I mentioned this to Bob, and he immediately got concerned and suggested I should take it more seriously.

He then used his influence to get me in to see one of the hospital's top docs that afternoon. The doctor examined me and gave me the news: I needed to have my gallbladder removed immediately. The surgery was scheduled for the next day. Now I needed to call Jackie and give her the news. This was not trivial. We lived an hour from the Washington Hospital Center, in Severna Park, Maryland. In addition, Jackie was seven months pregnant.

I went home and packed, and Jackie and I immediately drove back to Washington, and I checked in to the hospital. The place was awesome. We even got a separate bed in the room for Jackie to sleep on. There was no way she would be driving back to Maryland each night. Back in 1985 gallbladder surgery was performed with about an eight-inch incision. It was not done with a small incision and a scope, as it is now. This was a major event that kept me in the hospital for five days.

However, after the second day I was feeling well enough to start walking around. Of course I was in my hospital gown and had an IV attached to a rolling stand. But while recovering I had the opportunity to check on my evaluation devices. You see, they were installed just down the hall from my room, at the nursing station. Some sales folks will go to any extreme to win a deal!

Sometimes thinking outside the box involves a commitment from sales management. In the late '90s, with folks purchasing personal computers in droves and looking for access to the World Wide Web, business was flourishing for America Online (AOL). Consequently they had unprecedented demand to store content. Located in Northern Virginia, AOL was one of the accounts in our district. We had switched their account reps several times; it seemed that regardless of who represented EMC, AOL was not interested in changing data storage vendors. It was clear AOL represented the single largest opportunity for EMC not only on a district level but from a corporate prospective.

Then, in 1998, sales management at EMC had an epiphany: AOL required intense focus if it was to be cracked. Having AOL as part of a typical sales exec's territory was not a solid strategy. The reason was twofold:

1) A salesman at EMC had a very high quota. In addition EMC sales execs were measured on a quarterly basis. It was therefore important for them to target accounts they felt confident they could close in order to make their objectives. The amount of time invested in AOL would mean that time would be taken away from their efforts to hit their quarterly numbers. And EMC did not look favorably

on sales reps who missed their quarterly numbers several times in a row. As a result of this, not enough focus was given to AOL.

2) If AOL was to be cracked, it would require an investment of EMC's time and money. There needed to be intense focus and commitment by one senior-level sales exec in order to convert AOL to an EMC storage customer. Management had to make a conscious decision not to hold the rep on the AOL account to a quarterly sales objective. Additionally it would be necessary to dedicate a technical resource to support the sales exec. This was clearly "outside the box" thinking for a company that previously had been driven by quarterly sales objectives.

MJ, a senior sales exec, was hired at EMC and assigned to AOL as his only account. He was given Joel, an outstanding technical resource, to support his sales efforts. But he was still given a $9 million annual quota.

So how did MJ begin his sales campaign at AOL? He promptly reported to work every day — in the AOL cafeteria. Yes, he essentially set up his office there. Initially he had very few scheduled appointments. He did his best to learn the landscape of the company as well as the various technical and management folks by being onsite. He would have Joel do technical discussions and whiteboard presentations when time permitted. He became a permanent fixture there.

Additionally, he and Joel promoted an EMC happy hour at a local watering hole. They put flyers around the AOL cafeteria and in the men's rooms to advertise free beer complements of EMC. Initially only one person from AOL and three from EMC attended the happy hours. However, over time they grew, and the folks at AOL looked forward to them.

The EMC team and the AOL team began to connect. It was clear to MJ that he was making progress. He was given a small opportunity to provide storage for an HP server. This particular application was not for AOL's core business, but it was a welcomed start. EMC shipped and installed its first system in 1999. The technical team onsite at AOL made sure the system performed perfectly. MJ and his team socialized the success of this first installation and continued to press on for more opportunities.

The result of MJ's first full year at AOL was $1 million of a $9 million quota. EMC sales management was questioning whether they should pull the plug on this investment. They asked MJ if he wanted to continue. He had invested so much in the last twelve months and clearly wanted to press on. Somewhat reluctantly, EMC sales management gave MJ the go-ahead to continue. They did, however, apply pressure, as they are legendarily known to do.

Later that year MJ got a call from one of the senior folks at AOL, who asked if he could get two large data storage systems shipped and installed ASAP for a mission-critical database application. MJ and his technical team had spent a significant amount of selling time explaining how the EMC technology would be an excellent fit for database applications. It provided much better performance than the storage AOL was currently using.

This was the break MJ had been looking for. The systems were installed and performed as advertised. Not long after, AOL began ordering more and more storage from EMC.

By the end of 1999, AOL did $50 million in business with EMC. Based on a $9 million quota, MJ was the top sales exec at EMC that year. As one would expect, his quota was raised the next year. That's the price of success!

CHAPTER REVIEW

- Consider internal and external alternatives to conventional thinking.
- Focus on areas that will maximize your time and provide opportunities to make more sales calls.
- If possible, make it a team effort.
- Be creative.
- Challenge conventional wisdom.

CHAPTER 16

CAREER CHANGES BOTH IN AND OUT OF YOUR INDUSTRY

In 1986 I was interviewing for a sales job with the VP of sales of Thomas Nationwide Computer Corporation. The VP's name was Art. He had been brought in from Storage Technology Corporation to grow the company. In order do that, his mission was to look for sales reps who had relationships with IBM mainframe accounts in different parts of the country.

Art was a very polished executive who had previously run a very large sales organization at Storage Tech. We met in downtown Baltimore and had a great discussion about the opportunities in the computer leasing business as well as how it differed from representing a manufacturer. I had been with Telex Computer Products for about eight years at the time. My income for a thirty-two-year-old was higher than most, but quite frankly I was getting bored. I felt I needed a change to reenergize myself, and moving into the computer leasing business would allow me to move up to a higher level of professional sales. I would be dealing more at the executive level and would have to learn a lot of new skills around finance and leasing options. It was a big step because I was very comfortable and secure at Telex.

During lunch Art made a statement to me that I will never forget: "Your responsibility as a professional salesman is to be with the right company with the right product at the right time."

That statement has had a tremendous impact on me to this day. If you take the time to reflect on it the statement is obviously true, but do we all adhere to it? If in fact we make decisions to stay in sales long term. Shouldn't we be aware of the changing markets in our industries and reevaluate our current positions and opportunities?

Don't misunderstand me. I am by *no means* advocating annual job changes. We have all seen sales reps who are constantly changing jobs, looking for the big hit. This is counterproductive and will ultimately be detrimental to your career. What I am saying is that you should not place your head firmly in the sand and never evaluate other opportunities. Some folks get very comfortable and have blinders on, and convince themselves they need to stay because they have been there for so long. Or perhaps they are scared of change.

There is certainly nothing wrong with loyalty. It is a good thing. We just need to be careful not to take it to the extreme. And, most important, do we really know if the company would show loyalty to us? Just because you have been a valuable employee for fifteen years, do you really believe you have more value than someone they are paying less who has been with them for two years? When the rubber meets the road, corporate America will do what it needs to do to survive. And if it means taking out a number of long-term employees, you might be a casualty.

There is certainly value in staying with the same company as long as it is financially stable and continues to provide products and services your clients purchase. A key question to ask yourself is this: are your clients buying from you because you have a superior product or service, or are they buying primarily because of the relationship you have built over the years?

Are you losing ground to the competition? Or is the competition clearly offering a better alternative and you are heavily leaning on your business relationship to continue to win business? It is your responsibility to monitor the market and industry to ensure the product you represent remains competitive.

Think about it from another perspective. As a professional salesman you have spent many years earning trust and respect from your client base. They buy from you because they trust your recommendations and believe you will not steer them in the wrong direction. Perhaps in some cases they don't spend a lot of time evaluating the competition because they trust you and your company's product. You know your company is falling behind the competition, but you continue to do business because of the tight relationships you have with your clients.

At some point these clients will become aware that you and the company you represent have not kept pace with the industry. Or maybe they will find out that your product is overpriced. Regardless of the specific details, the fact is your client will feel you took advantage of the business relationship. It will be hard to recover from this scenario, especially if your product is inferior and overpriced.

As a professional you are supposed to have your clients' best interests in mind. You are supposed to be the trusted advisor who does not take advantage of a relationship for selfish purposes. It takes years to build trust and respect. Unfortunately they can be taken away in an instant. Protect these valuable commodities buy monitoring the industry you sell in and the competitive landscape. You want to be proud of the product and company you represent. If this changes it is your responsibility to evaluate your options and determine which company and product will serve your client base the best. In other words the client base is the constant; the company you represent may change based on a variety of circumstances.

A decision to leave one company and move on to another should not be undertaken lightly. And it never should be done for money only. For example if you have an excellent reputation for representing a product in a given territory, you are in fact a valuable commodity to a competitor. You will most likely receive calls from executive recruiters or directly from competitors with job offers. They want you because of your experience and, most importantly, your strong client relationships.

Some of these offers will be very attractive. That is why it is critical to evaluate them thoroughly from much more than a monetary standpoint. Evaluate the offers from your *clients'* perspectives. If you do, the offer has a better chance of standing the test of time. We make money in sales based on how much revenue we generate. So it stands to reason that we would need to sell a new product to our existing client base. If the new product will not withstand the test of time, it might not be a good long-term fit for your current client base. If this is the case, I would be careful about making a move. This is sometimes the case with new or startup companies that want to leverage *your* relationships for *their* advantage.

EMC used this strategy in the early '90s. It was an absolutely brilliant strategy. At the time EMC developed and manufactured groundbreaking data storage technology. It was far superior to IBM in terms of performance, reliability, power savings, and floor space. EMC executives were smart, but having groundbreaking technology does not make a successful company. *Selling* groundbreaking technology is the key. It sounds simple but *nothing* happens until something is sold.

EMC executives knew they needed to get this technology in front of decision maker's at large IBM mainframe installations. And they needed to do it fast before IBM had sufficient time to react. The best way to attain immediate access to key IBM data center decisions makers was to hire sales reps who had these relationships. At that time IBM had enjoyed about an 80 percent market share in mainframe data storage. Three other companies split the other 20 percent: Hitachi Data Systems, Storage Technology, and Memorex/Telex (MTC). To attain access to the sales reps, EMC hired sales managers from these three companies. The sales managers then recruited their top performers.

These sales folks had typically been calling on senior management at large IBM data centers for many years. They had the relationships EMC needed in order to attain immediate access. When successful sales reps at HDS, STK, and MTC were exposed to this revolutionary EMC technology, they knew their existing clients would benefit. They knew EMC was so far superior to the IBM offerings that once their client base was exposed to it they would never purchase any more IBM storage. It was a match made in heaven. EMC needed access to IBM data storage decision makers, and the sales execs who had those relationships were excited about representing this new technology.

In 1993 I was working at Memorex/Telex. Our primary focus was tape systems. We did have data storage, but it did not stack up well against the competition. Additionally, MTC was having some financial issues, and it was becoming increasingly difficult to represent the company and product to my client base. I had done some research and found out that EMC had developed new technology based on a small form factor disc drive. They also had written some software that staged I/Os from mainframe applications in cache memory, which significantly improved performance. This was a departure from traditional storage systems, and therefore EMC did not have a very large installed base.

Additionally, in many cases, it takes years to gain a footprint in large IBM data centers. So even with this new and exciting technology, it wasn't surprising that EMC did not have many systems installed. Several senior sales execs had left Memorex/Telex to join EMC about a year prior. I contacted each of them to discuss his success in selling the product as well as the support after the sale. In many cases the service and support after the sale are just as important as the performance of the data storage itself. If it breaks and the service reps can't repair it in a timely fashion, the performance will be of little value.

During these discussions I found that not only did their clients love the performance, but the service and support was, in many cases, superior to IBM's. The EMC data storage had a "call home" feature that called the EMC support center in Hopkinton, Massachusetts, to alert the home office that a component was failing. The technician was then dispatched to the account *before* the component failed. I also found out that many of the field service technicians were former Memorex/Telex field service engineers.

And since most of the components in the system were redundant, the uptime was predicted to be higher than the current IBM data storage.

So it looked to me like EMC not only had technology that was superior to IBM's but also superior reliability and service. After speaking with the sales execs, I spoke with several clients I had strong relationships with to get their takes on EMC. Most told me it sounded like very interesting technology and they would welcome the opportunity to learn more. The EMC reps had confirmed that the company and the product were first class, and that their clients were delighted. My client base confirmed they would be interested in evaluating EMC as an alternative to IBM. All things were pointing to the fact that EMC would offer an excellent opportunity to land in light of the current issues at MTC.

All of the research confirmed an excellent opportunity for Scott Dunkel at EMC. The only problem was I didn't have a job offer. So I took it upon myself to contact Al, the regional sales manager. He had responsibility from New York to Richmond at the time. I was interested in selling in the Baltimore/Washington, DC area. That was where I had my business relationships.

The good news was I had worked for Al several years earlier at Memorex/Telex, where I was the regional leasing manager and later, when the company downsized, a sales exec. When I spoke with Al, he told me EMC was looking to add a sales exec in the Baltimore office. I would need to interview with the district manager, Stu, who had responsibility for Baltimore and DC.

When I met with Stu it didn't really feel like an interview. He'd obviously gotten a good report from Al. Stu had started his career with IBM then moved to Hitachi Data Systems, and had been with EMC for about a year at the time of our interview. Stu basically asked me when I could start to work. So now the only thing left to discuss was the compensation plan. EMC's at the time was very generous, so that part turned out to be easy.

The point is to do the necessary homework on the company's product as well as the company's long-term viability. Then determine how your existing client base will respond to you representing a new company. You've spent a long time developing these client relationships. It would be unfortunate not to take advantage of them.

What about evaluating opportunities outside of your industry? This of course is much more difficult for various reasons:

1) You are not as familiar with all of the potential players in a new industry.
2) You don't have client relationships to leverage.
3) You have to learn all the nuances of a new industry.

There may be good reason to make a move to another industry. Perhaps yours is dying. Or perhaps you just don't enjoy selling the product or service anymore and you need a change. Maybe your industry simply doesn't pay well. The fact of the matter is certain industries pay more than others. You could be one of the top performers in the sports apparel field and you might not earn as much as an average performer in the high tech field. This is a fact of life. It might not have anything to do with talent.

As a professional sales exec it is your responsibility to seek out the industries that pay the most. That is if income is the most critical component of the job. It's like deciding you want to be a waiter or waitress for the next five years. Would you seek employment at Ruth's Chris Steak House or at Denny's? You are in charge of your destiny. Make a conscious choice regarding the industry and companies where you seek employment.

On the other hand if your life dream is to sell golf clubs or tennis racquets; then you will have to deal with the compensation plans at these companies. In the best of both worlds you would find a product you love to sell for a company that offers an outstanding compensation plan. On the other hand, don't sell a product you hate with a company that has a poor compensation plan. That wouldn't make any sense.

So let's say you have decided to make a move outside of your industry. Your approach will be somewhat similar to a move within your industry. The difference is you will need to do a lot more homework and research. The first thing I would do is find a successful salesperson in that industry and buy her lunch. Learn as much as you can about the landscape. Who are the industry leaders? What are the challenges? Which company's market share is growing and which is losing ground?

Based on the information you receive you can then go to the web for further research. Narrow it down to a few companies you would like to work for. Now the real work begins. You need to get an interview with these companies' sales managers. And the fact that you don't have industry experience will make it a bit more challenging. Approach it as if you are selling a product or service to a typical prospect. The difference is you are selling *yourself.*

Get in touch with a sales rep who works for the sales manager. Explain your situation. If possible meet with a few sales reps who work for the manager. Learn as much as you can about him, the company, the competition, etc. Be a sponge. Suck up as much knowledge and information as you can. Learn as much as you can about the culture of the organization and the management style of the sales manager. Continue to do research on the Web in conjunction with the meetings with the sales reps. Become as much of an expert on the industry and the company as you can without working there. This is not a one-week project. It could take several months. However, if you've decided this is the company that will offer you the best future, you should put the same effort into it as you would a major selling opportunity.

When you have assembled this data, you are prepared to set up a meeting with the sales manager. Incidentally, you may want to run parallel efforts with two potential companies. The industry data in terms of the competition, market share, industry challenges, etc. will be the same. The only difference will be the approach with each sales manager, which will differ based on the G2 you gleaned from the discussions with the sales folks who work for them.

So go ahead and set up meetings with two sales managers since you have done all of this research. Send them each a very detailed note describing why you would like to discuss a sales position with his company. It should be laced with specific data that could be learned only through exhaustive research. Tell each manager you are seeking employment with only a select number of companies in the industry. Explain why this field and the company excite you. Have some very specific questions that you would like to discuss with him. Send the letter, and follow up in a few days.

If this is done properly, you will have no problem getting the interview. But, most importantly, all of your research will prepare you for the interview like no one else. The manager will be very impressed by the knowledge you have even though you don't actually work in the industry. You will demonstrate an astounding desire to be successful in a new industry. In some cases you might have more useful industry data than some of the reps who currently work for them. Many times reps get stale and lose energy. Your ability to offer a fresh look as an outsider might be a welcomed addition to the sales team. Remember, there is no substitute for enthusiasm! This is particularly true in the field of professional sales.

In the interview don't be afraid to discuss your logic and methodology for pursuing this opportunity. The manager would be foolish to view it as anything other than inspiring with a hint of aggressiveness. If you are willing to go to this length to position yourself for a positive interview, then it stands to reason you would pursue normal business opportunities the same way. If it turns out there are no immediate sales opportunities available, don't be discouraged. Your research and knowledge will position you for other interviews in this industry. Remember, this is a marathon, not a sprint.

Throughout my career I witnessed many professional sales execs migrating to IT sales from other industries. There were folks from the medical sales field, the wholesale glass industry, and the office products field to name a few. Learning a new product and industry does require a ramp-up period but can be accomplished in a reasonable amount of time with the proper focus and energy. The fact that you most likely will not be able to call on the same clients is more of a disadvantage in my opinion.

In my interviews with senior sales managers I asked if they would prefer to hire an excellent sales exec from another field or an average sales exec in their field. The resounding answer was they would prefer to have sales excellence and train, as opposed to the latter. Product knowledge and industry knowledge can be learned. Work ethic, interpersonal skills, and integrity are more difficult to find.

CHAPTER REVIEW:

- Review your present company, product, income, and future on an annual basis.
- Don't put your head in the sand by not being open-minded about other opportunities.
- Changing industries offers a multitude of possibilities.
- Before making *any* change, do your homework—these decisions should not be taken lightly.
- Avoid making too many sales job changes.
- A successful sales exec with a robust client base is a valuable commodity!

CHAPTER 17

PUTTING IT ALL TOGETHER

In order to position yourself for a successful career as a sales exec, one would assume you should take the time to learn how senior executives prefer to be called on. After all if you gain this wisdom, your chances of doing business with your prospects will be increased significantly.

I took the time to interview senior executives at major corporations in order to glean this knowledge. By adhering to these truths you will not only improve your chances of success but, equally importantly, the folks you call on will appreciate your professionalism and as a result enjoy the business relationship. You will be viewed as someone who doesn't waste their time and only advances proposals that add value and solve legitimate business issues. Additionally, if you change companies you will always be welcomed back to discuss potential solutions your new company might offer.

The attributes senior executives look for in professional sales execs are discussed in detail throughout this book. I thought it would be helpful to summarize them in this chapter. They can't be over emphasized.

- Integrity and character are paramount.
- Deliver on your promises.
- Stay in touch after the sale — don't just be around when business is on the table.
- Provide business solutions, not product features and benefits.
- Don't waste their valuable time.

There is one point I hope I made clearly in this book: a professional sales exec cannot reach his maximum potential alone! When you deposit your commission check, the teller doesn't ask if you earned the money without any assistance. She doesn't ask if you used various resources to close business and maybe gained an unfair competitive advantage. She certainly doesn't ask if you built a strong relationship with your client. She simply takes your check and deposits it in your account. No questions asked.

So you should use every possible tool in your bag to maximize your productivity. There is *no need* to do it on your own, just like life in general. We were created to develop relationships with other human beings. This is what separates the human race from animals.

A salesperson has both internal and external relationships. In this book we primarily focused on the external relationships with our prospects and clients. We know that the stronger the relationship we build in terms of trust and respect, the better the chance of winning the business. But what about the internal relationships? These are what we forge with the folks in our company. They can make a huge difference in your success as well. Since sales should be a team effort, it is *your* responsibility as the leader to build strong internal relationships. Be the sales exec folks want to go out of their way to help. Don't be the rep people run the other way from when they see you coming down the hall. We've all known the person who thinks the world revolves around him. He *demands* that things get done instead of asking politely. He talks behind people's backs and throws everyone under the bus — except the person he is presently talking to. He is so full of himself, his ego comes in the room a few seconds before he does, and he leaves a negative wake in almost every encounter. And, when he loses a deal, it's everyone's fault except his.

I have witnessed several such abrasive sales reps in my career. And in some cases they have been successful in terms of quota attainment. But this type of behavior eventually catches up with them. Treating your coworkers with respect and dignity is the right way to operate. And it will make time spent in the office much more enjoyable! Enough said about what not to do. You get the point.

At Memorex/Telex and EMC, the two companies where I spent the lion's share of my career, it was always a team effort. The successful sales execs leveraged the strengths of their teams and made sure the teams were recognized for their efforts. These were very technical sales, so it was critical to have strong technical resources available. Many times the difference between winning and losing a deal was directly related to the strength of the technical resources, so it was important to let them know how much they were appreciated. And when you won a deal, the resources' manager should know how instrumental they were in securing the business. Share the joy! Don't make it all about you.

The same principle holds true for customer engineers. These are the folks who install, diagnose, upgrade, and repair the systems we sell. They are the guys who do the installs in the middle of the night, who get the call at 3:00 a.m. when a system goes down. They need some love too.

At the end of the day, if your service organization is weak, it significantly diminishes your chances of doing more business. So take the time to share your success with the service folks as well. Give them tickets to a ball game once in a while. Buy them lunch on occasion. Let them know they are appreciated. Meet them while they're doing an install and bring them coffee and donuts—perhaps even at an install that is after hours. It will go a long way toward building a solid relationship.

How about your administrative support? These are the folks who put your orders in the system. Perhaps they have some interaction with your clients. You might need them to stay late one night to process an order. They're part of your team as well. Make sure they feel appreciated.

The same holds true for all of the folks at headquarters with whom you have interactions. Treat them well. Be kind and uplifting in your interactions. Tell them how much you appreciate their efforts. In some cases these folks will have direct impacts on your success. Be mindful of this and give them the respect they — and, for that matter, everyone — deserve.

IS THIS REALLY WORK?

Believe it or not, I would get just as excited about making a quality sales call as I did about playing a round of golf or riding my motorcycle. Granted, I might be the exception, but I truly believe most successful sales execs get tremendous excitement from conducting successful sales campaigns, which ultimately leads to generating profitable sales.

As we have discussed, a successful call does not happen by accident. It is born out of asking the right questions and being a good listener, and then presenting *exactly* and *precisely* what your prospect needs. This is essential for a quality sales call. And when you continually bring value to your client, you become an essential partner — one who is trusted and respected.

In my interviews with decision makers, it was made clear to me that they *want* to have valued partners. Evaluating vendors on a constant basis is time consuming and, for many, not very enjoyable. They would prefer to have a few partners they can trust and not have to go through a negotiation or bid process for every deal. They are looking for someone like *you*. So do your best not to let them down.

LET THE FUN BEGIN!

Once you become a trusted partner, there is a definite blur between business and pleasure. You will be invited to certain company events to which other vendors do not receive invitations. Additionally, you will be given access to senior executives because of the way you are now viewed. Many times you will be asked to attend meetings to which only strategic partners are privy. And you will find yourself spending a lot more time out of the office with your client. Perhaps this will be on the golf course, tennis court, or ski slope, or at a nice restaurant. You will ask yourself on many occasions, "Is this business or pleasure?"

However, I must caution you. Just because you have elevated your company and yourself to this elite level of trusted advisor, you cannot and should not take it lightly. Your objective is to continue to provide the same level of service that earned you the position. You must be careful not to take shortcuts in your selling activities. It is critical not to take advantage of this relationship by assuming you will get all the business by just showing up. Remember, there are competitors out there. Many are very skilled and successful sales execs who are working behind the scenes to gain a foothold in your account. It should be your business never to assume you will be awarded a contract. You have worked long and hard to get to this position. Don't throw it all away by not being proactive in every business opportunity.

As you have come to realize, this is not a book of *sales tactics*. There are tons of those out there if you need help in that area. I wrote this book to help professional sales execs accelerate their careers and have fun doing it. At the end of the day, it boils down to a three-step process:

Understand your client's business and challenges.

Ask relevant questions and *listen* carefully to the responses.

Apply your solution to the client's issue.

Of course this is an oversimplification of the art of professional selling. However, it is the basis of any successful sales

WHAT THEY DON'T TEACH YOU IN SALES SCHOOL

campaign. What separates the great reps from the average reps is the *execution* of this universal truth. Knowing what to do and knowing how to do it successfully are two different things.

The universal sales truths I refer to are high-level core principles that I believe will positively influence your sales success and make your life simpler and less stressful. If you adhere to these principles, people in general will tend to like, trust, and respect you. In the discussions I've had with my previous clients, they *all* have valued these three attributes and consequently wanted to do business with these folks.

So make it a point to seek out the sales execs both within and outside your company who reflect these attributes. You will typically find they are the most successful and the most respected. Learn from them. In most cases they will be happy to mentor you. There is great joy and satisfaction in sharing the wisdom they have gleaned through the years.

Successful people love to talk about their past success and share mistakes they have made. You will be the beneficiary of all this wisdom. Just as you do with your prospects, when learning from successful sales folks spend more time listening! Ask good questions and then sit back and listen carefully. If you are there for advice, allow your mentor to dominate the conversation. This is not the time for you to talk about how good you are. There is an old saying that goes something like this: What would you rather do? Receive a gift of $10,000 or learn how to make $10,000? Would you rather be given a fish or learn how to fish for yourself? In other words wisdom and knowledge is much more valuable than a onetime gift or windfall.

Additionally, be mindful of the folks you associate with. Make it a point to socialize with and learn from folks in your organization who will uplift you and provide sound and wise advice. Don't get caught up in the office gossip and consequently find yourself in negative conversations that will bring you down. Wise people associate with wise people. Dumb people associate with not so wise people.

In all conversations chose your words wisely. Words can either build up or break down a relationship. There is no better way to sabotage a long-term business relationship then to speak harshly out of emotion. Whether it is in person, on the phone, or via e-mail or texting, in emotionally charged situations take a deep breath before you respond. Once it is out of your mouth or you press "send," there is no turning back.

Probably the most important universal sales truth is to continue to work your land. Like a farmer, if you don't continue to plant seeds, eventually you will have nothing to harvest. This is not a sprint! It is a marathon. The sales execs who are the most successful continue to execute on their annual business plans. This is especially true when things are not going so great. It's very easy to stay pumped up when you are ahead of quota and the talk of the office. But it is even more important to keep a positive attitude and continue to work your plan when things are not going well. This is what separates the true professionals from the rest of the pack.

APPENDIX: FIVE UNIVERSAL SALES TRUTHS

1) *Surround yourself with successful people of integrity.*

Proverbs 13:20
Become wise by walking with the wise;
hang out with fools and watch your life fall to pieces.

Proverbs 15:22
Refuse good advice and watch your plans fail;
take good counsel and watch them succeed.

Proverbs 16:16
Get wisdom — it's worth more than money;
choose insight over income every time.

Proverbs 19:9
The person who tells lies gets caught;
the person who spreads rumors is ruined.

Proverbs 28:26
If you think you know it all, you're a fool for sure;
real survivors learn wisdom from others.

2) *Use your words carefully — think* **before responding!**

Proverbs 12:16
Fools have short fuses and explode all too quickly;
the prudent quietly shrug off insults.

Proverbs 12:18
Rash language cuts and maims,
but there is healing in the words of the wise.

Proverbs 13:3
Careful words make for a careful life;
careless talk may ruin everything.

Proverbs 14:29
Slowness to anger makes for deep understanding;
a quick-tempered person stockpiles stupidity.

Proverbs 18:21
Words kill, words give life;
they're either poison or fruit — you choose.

3) *Do more listening than talking.*

Proverbs 18:13
Answering before listening
is both stupid and rude.

4) *Work your land.*

Proverbs 20:4
A farmer too lazy to plant in the spring
has nothing to harvest in the fall.

Proverbs 28:19-20
Work your garden — you'll end up with plenty of food;
play and party — you'll end up with an empty plate.

Committed and persistent work pays off;
get-rich-quick schemes are rip-offs.

5) *Be humble, not prideful.*

Proverbs 11:2
The stuck-up fall flat on their faces,
but down-to-earth people stand firm.

Proverbs 23:5
Cast but a glance at riches, and they are gone.
And they will surely sprout wings
And fly off to the sky like an eagle.

ABOUT THE AUTHOR

After graduating from St. John's University in 1976 with a degree in business administration, Scott Dunkel accepted a position as a sales representative with Burroughs Corporation. He was assigned a territory in Brooklyn, New York, that included sections of Bedford-Stuyvesant, East New York, Brownsville, Greenpoint, and Williamsburg. For those of you who know New York, you can appreciate how challenging this territory was back in the '70s.

After two years of pounding the Brooklyn pavement selling mini-computers and high-end business calculators, Scott recognized his efforts would be better served by representing another product in another market. His research uncovered an excellent opportunity to sell plug-compatible devices for IBM mainframe computers with a company called Telex Computer Products. The company was transitioning from selling tape and disk drives to 3270-compatible display terminals. The mainframe world was going online, which generated significant demand for terminal displays, and IBM could not keep up with the demand. Telex was positioned to capitalize on this demand and was looking to add a sales rep in New York City.

Scott contacted Frank, Telex's regional sales manager, to discuss the opportunity. The conversation did not go well. Frank was interested in a more seasoned sales exec — one who was in his thirties or forties and had a minimum of ten years of successfully competing against IBM in the mainframe market. Scott had a year and half of experience selling mini-computers door to door in Brooklyn. He was not what Frank was looking for.

But Scott's lack of experience was offset by his tenacity and never-say-die attitude. He continued to contact Frank on a monthly basis and met him several times. Additionally, Scott found out that Frank was a huge tennis fan and consequently arranged to take him and his wife, Linda, to the US Open. At the time Scott's fiancé worked for the United States Tennis Association.

Scott approached his pursuit of the Telex sales opportunity much like a professional sales exec would sell to a major account. After almost a year of intense selling, Scott was finally offered the job in July 1978. At the time Telex had only thirty sales folks in the entire country. Scott was the youngest at twenty-four. All of the other reps were in their mid- to late thirties. Some were approaching fifty! This was truly a very seasoned and professional sales force that needed very little management.

Scott's new territory was a bit of an upgrade from what he covered at Burroughs. He was assigned the entire city of New York as well as Long Island. Lots of IBM mainframes equaled lots of opportunity. The challenge for Scott was his lack of experience, which Frank had felt was necessary in order to be successful at Telex. Additionally, since Telex was a small company, they didn't have sales or product training. Employees were expected to do everything on their own. Scott had convinced Frank that he could do the job — now he had to execute on that promise.

Scott spent eight successful years with Telex, learning how to be a professional sales exec from some of the best in the industry. In 1986 Thomas Nationwide Computer Corporation offered him an opportunity to learn the computer leasing business. He took the job and learned a lot about the financial aspects of business, but it did not sit well with him. He spent three years in the leasing business before ultimately accepting a position back at Telex, which had merged with Memorex, as the mid-Atlantic regional leasing manager.

In 1993, with Memorex/Telex struggling financially from the debt service that resulted from the merger, Scott began to look for other opportunities. As luck would have it, his previous manager at Memorex/Telex had landed a successful position at EMC Corporation. Al had sales responsibility for the entire mid-Atlantic region. And the good news was EMC was looking to add a rep in the Baltimore/Washington, DC area. Scott contacted Al and began his twelve-year career with EMC.

During his career at EMC, Scott consistently attained quota and replaced IBM data storage with EMC in more than twenty accounts in the Baltimore/Washington, DC area. He was responsible for placing the first EMC storage systems in accounts such as Citigroup, Blue Cross, T. Rowe Price, World Bank, GEICO, First Data, and Allegis Group.

In the field of high-technology sales, an industry infamous for churning and burning sales reps, Scott mastered the craft of professional sales for more than twenty-five years. In this book he shares insightful examples from his career that will resonate with sales folks competing at the highest levels.

Today Scott focuses his attention on helping sales professionals elevate their game to new levels by offering workshops as well as one-on-one sales mentoring. Additionally, he volunteers his time with SCORE, a nonprofit association affiliated with the Small Business Association. SCORE is dedicated to helping small businesses get off the ground, grow, and achieve their goals through education and mentorship.

For more information on sales mentoring and consulting or to purchase additional copies of the book please go to www.universalsalestruths.com

Printed in Great Britain
by Amazon.co.uk, Ltd.,
Marston Gate.